THE PHOENIX AND THE ASHES

BY THE SAME AUTHOR

IRAN'S SECRET POGROM – THE CONSPIRACY TO WIPE
OUT THE BAHÁ'ÍS (Neville Spearman)

THE PHOENIX AND THE ASHES

The Bahá'í Faith
and the Modern Apocalypse

by

GEOFFREY NASH

GEORGE RONALD

OXFORD

GEORGE RONALD, Publisher
46 High Street, Kidlington, Oxford, OX5 2DN

ISBN 0–85398–199–X (softcover)

Printed and bound in Great Britain at
The Camelot Press Ltd, Southampton

Contents

Preface   vii

The Lost Hope of the Nineteenth Century   1

From Vision to Nightmare   36

The Bahá'í Faith and the Philosophy of History   66

The Bahá'í Faith and Political Theory   104

The Modern Apocalypse   124

Postscript   144

Select Bibliography   147

TO ROGER WHITE

in admiration and affection

Preface

This series of essays looks back over the two hundred years separating our time from the French Revolution and the great era of change with which it is synchronized, and attempts to delineate a pattern. Historians do this most of the time – for the writing of history, as opposed to mere chronicling, involves the conscious selection of facts and details, trends and ideas. As Strachey wrote of the Victorian age:

. . . our fathers and grandfathers have poured forth and accumulated so vast a quantity of information that the industry of a Ranke would be submerged by it, and the perspicacity of a Gibbon would quail before it. It is not by the direct method of a scrupulous narration that the explorer of the past can hope to depict that singular epoch.

Preface to Eminent Victorians, London, 1918

Strachey proposed rowing over the ocean of material and here and there lowering a little bucket and then examining its contents. The opposite method has been adopted here: an overall pattern is suggested, what the jargon calls an 'overview', in the hope of making sense of the entire period.

Of course such a method is speculative and subjective, and, many would maintain, bad history; all the writer can plead is that his case be allowed a hearing. What he intends to draw is a picture of revolutionary changes in the last century accompanied by the expectation of a new age. The failure of this expectation to materialize, the absence of renewal and the continuation of decline and disintegration, are studied in the light of Bahá'í belief in a spiritual rebirth that began in the last century, and is working through our own times, albeit still unperceived by the mass of humanity.

This book, then, is a mixture of literary history, political history, philosophy of history, and religion. I apologize to the reader in advance for this pot-pourri, and can but hope that through the mixture of disciplines he may grasp something of the path of search I have embarked upon.

For here I have endeavoured to face and respond to a series of questions that have long interested me. They may be phrased in the following way, without by any means exhausting the range of issues discussed in this book:

1. Why were men far more hopeful about the destiny of mankind in 1850 than they are today?

2. How can we account for the lurch into hopelessness of much of modern civilization in the twentieth century?

3. Where is humanity heading, and what are the immediate prospects of the human race?

4. Is there any organization, agency, or school of thought that can help canalize the desire for spiritual renewal that so many people feel?

Many will be alienated by the conclusions I reach. Some will take issue with my dismissal of the established, traditional religions; others will quarrel with my attitude to political action. But there will be also some, I hope, who will be willing to accept the possibility that radical problems require a solution more radical than any the current religious or political systems are ready to provide. The presupposition that I have made, and which the reader must follow if the book is to have any value for him, is that the above questions *can* be answered; that in fact the universe and history do yield rational as well as suprarational answers to the searching mind of man; and that although we live in a world of chaos and confusion, there is beneath this a universal order that man is capable of reflecting in himself as well as in his society.

I may say that I started out with the disposition to accept the pessimism of this time, and to see our age as a blighted one: but the conclusion of my search led me to believe, without denying the tragic dimension to the twentieth century, that renewal is also working through a dark period in human history, so that one may still echo in hope the German Romantic, Richter: 'Infinite Providence, Thou wilt cause the day to dawn . . .'

Geoffrey Nash

London, August 1984

The Lost Hope of the Nineteenth Century

I

THE FRENCH REVOLUTION and the forces that re-shaped European society between 1780 and 1850 came as a revelation to those who lived through them. The French Revolution itself presided over the whole age as the greatest single factor behind the inauguration of the new era. It was not merely a political event, or even the destruction of an old order; it was a new advent, the point of genesis of a new age and a new world.

The new revelation had its social and political aspect, and its spiritual and metaphysical. At first, in the heady days of the Romantic era, political revolutions were staged with haphazard abandonment, and the new age was intended to result in the dethronement of tyranny and the establishment of liberty in which all would partake. It seemed needful only to spread the new gospel, raise the barricades and give one's life for the new millennium to be achieved. There was brutality and massacre enough in this ideal struggle to prophesy the débâcles to come, although at the time participants were mainly students and army officers, poets and educated artisans. Meanwhile, in the lofty world of idealist philosophy, the French Revolution had already been canonized. Fichte enthusiastically welcomed the advance of the revolutionary French armies, although he would later switch his allegiance to German nationalism.

What was apparent to the philosophers was that the process of change and reconstruction had only begun in France. There remained a new order to originate. To the technocrat turned mystic, Saint-Simon, the prospect of creating a new order and, as he came to demand, a new religion, required the inspiration of a prophet. He was one of the first, but by no means the last, to adopt the mantle himself.

The new environment led some to speak of higher revelations. Religious enthusiasts discovered themselves to be the vehicles of a Second Coming, while others searched their Bibles and discovered the imminent return of the Lord and the rule of the saints.

The new conditions of the early nineteenth century inspired many to try to read the signs of the times, to arise and fulfil the exigencies as they understood them, of a new time. And in their interpretations and theses a consciousness of a historical millennium achieving fruition in their own age was not far to seek. Expectancy and hope were generated: this age was a momentous one in which to be alive, all other times were envious of this one; to live now was thus to gain a portion of immortality when future men would look back in envy to that great dawn.

The Romantic Ingredient

The Romantic movement in Europe held sway to as late perhaps as 1850. We account it a wonderfully rich period in the thought and culture of the continent. Supreme works of art still testify to the fecundity of the Romantic spirit. A new life stirred in the soul of Europe and left behind the great symphonies of Beethoven, Schubert and Mendelssohn, the *Faust* of Goethe and the lyric poetry of his compatriot contemporaries; not to speak of the novels of Scott, Manzoni and Balzac, the canvases of Turner, Delacroix and Gericault, and the philosophical and historical works of Schiller, Schelling, Schlegel, Fichte and Carlyle. And there was still more besides in arguably the most important creative period in Europe since the Renaissance.

Yet of course the Romantics are not accorded immunity from criticism on account of their genius – for they bequeathed a heritage, and upon their shoulders has been laid the blame for sowing the seeds of revolution, disorder, individualism, neuroticism, and many other evils of the later age and ours. That they lived intensely is not to be denied – only, it is countered, they lived prodigally, egotistically, amorally. Can we then countenance their praise, or go as far as to endorse many of their most characteristic beliefs?

Indeed, what the Romantics 'believed' suggests at least a homogeneity and at most a creed, and this much they did not possess – according to some. After all, some were Catholics, some Protestant, some pantheist, others even atheist – what could they hold in common?

In their rejection of the eighteenth-century mechanistic view of life the Romantics, from the conservative Scott to the revolutionary Kleist, were one. The work of the two writers named displays a similar rejection of rational control as the basis of a rich life. It is not surprising that such a rejection of rationality should lead to diverse experience involving violence and suicide, mysticism and intercourse with the supernatural, advocacy of the imaginative and intuitive faculties, sensuality, repentance, conversion, ecstasy, guilt and melancholia. Some indeed died young, but some too died like Wordsworth, in Arnold's words, grown old in 'an age he contemned'.

Inherent in all this was an individualism which all the great Romantics shared. They were slaves to no traditional code unless, as in the case of Friedrich Schlegel, the path they had taken to get there had been remarkably singular. Indeed, without the comfort of an insulating orthodoxy, the Romantics took to rediscovering the world anew, to exploring the life of the soul outside of any church, coming to struggle with their own spirit of truth.

Such a course was turbulent and often tragic. The Romantic vision was exhilarating but fragmented, and the ultimate goal was rarely reached this side of the grave. Yet that Romantic soul, which so often in hindsight appears only self-consuming and impractical, established this one important principle sadly lost in the constricting specialized views of the world that followed. That principle was search, and an openness to truth: no avenues were cut off because they were 'unrealistic', 'mythical', 'illusory', still less 'disproved'. For who had proved the idea in question false if he did not first experience it for himself? The Romantics were sceptics and agnostics in the best sense: they defied abstraction, compulsion and creeds which they held were barriers to the life of the soul; both the religion of the *ancien régime* and the scoffing of the *Philosophes* were anathema to them, because in both reality was compassed by formulas that inspired no life, only the lip-service of party men.

As long as this principle of individual discovery could be maintained in the face of an often sceptical world, the individual Romantic had life and purpose. The Schlegel brothers went in pursuit of the Middle Ages, discovered the heroic poetry of their pagan German ancestors, and proceeded to plumb the secrets of Sanskrit and of Oriental myth. Goethe found a spiritual ancestor in the Persian poet Hafiz; Herder ranged the languages and customs of the world, throwing new insight into the pedigrees of the different tribes of men. Later, Thomas Carlyle shot a beam of light across the phenomenon of Islam, and awoke European thought from ten centuries of ignorance and bigotry in his advocacy of Muhammad.

Within the pure disciplines of expression the voyage of discovery found new oceans: the transformation of the symphonic form by Beethoven, his late chamber works, the emotional journeys of Schubert and Schumann, the nature-worship of the English Romantics, and the religious visions of Blake and Novalis. All such travels in pursuit of perfect expression, insight and understanding were undertaken on the wings of inspiration – without it nought of exceptional worth could be achieved: the Romantic conception of the artist assumed the highest qualities, and none was able to work if he had the sense of being merely an artisan. The Romantic historian must also be artist and prophet, the philosopher must embrace the messianic role. If the sentiments were often bizarre and extravagant, when the *dramatis persona* was Balzac, Mickiewicz or Berlioz the subject in question had some genius to be extravagant about.

The inspirational aspect of Romanticism lent it a transcendental dimension which the sceptical have often labelled escapist or day-dream. The aim was frankly to raise men, to engender in them conscience and imaginative sympathy. Such ends could not be achieved by intolerance or proscription of whole areas of behaviour. The Enlightenment prescribed for God his limits, or excluded him altogether; it deprecated poetry and banished deep emotion. Romantics worked in the belief that men were better nourished through their spiritual and imaginative faculties than their analytical; that appeal was necessary to the rarely experienced deeper nature rather than the everyday 'common sense' part of men. The result in a given work of art thus depended on the participant in it – whether he was to consider it a diversion from the ordinary 'real' world, or to have his experience enlarged and his latent capacities awakened.

That a transcendent dimension actually existed was the burden of much Romantic art. But it must be admitted that the terms used by Romantic artists were often vague, revealing once more their aspiration of search rather than the certitude of knowledge. The looseness and airiness of Shelley's symbols is a case in point. The visionary world of Blake is in contrast replete with hidden meaning but available to hardly anyone but the visionary himself. Language might have been to blame, although the richness of natural and organic imagery invoked by many Romantic artists shows no lack of facility. The problem was that where the artist was visionary, priest and hero in the revealing of the unseen world, the burden of revelation became too much even for the genius to maintain. And in the loss of the sense of transcendent vision lay the secret of the inner disquietude of men like Coleridge and Carlyle.

The New Age motif first appears in Romantic poetry of the late eighteenth century, drawing its inspiration from the great hope of liberty and freedom generated by the French Revolution.

Thus Wordsworth:

> Bliss was it in that dawn to be alive
> And to be young was very heaven . . .

The ideal of brotherhood, and the sense of a new day in which all mankind partook, occurs in Schiller's famous 'Ode to Joy':

> O you millions, let me embrace you!
> Let this kiss be for the whole world!
> Brothers, above the tent of stars
> a loving Father cannot but dwell.

Goethe echoed this spirit of universalism in his *West–Eastern Divan*, from which the following lines come:

> To God belongs the Orient
> To God belongs the Occident,
> Northern lands and Southern lands
> Rest in the peace of His Hands.

English Romantic poets, Blake and Shelley in particular, sang their vision of a world transformed from the old tyranny into a loftier age, albeit not before a final upheaval between light and darkness in which darkness would be overcome (so Shelley's *Prometheus Unbound*; and throughout Blake's *Prophecies*).

The poets responded in part to events they lived through, and in part to new philosophical ideas such as those of Condorcet, Lessing and Kant, who all believed in progress toward a perfect human society. In part too, no doubt, the poets were thrilled by some unseen commotion in the universal consciousness of mankind – a quotient still imperfectly understood, though perhaps more respectable to serious thought after the beginning of psychology, and notably the work of Jung.

But exhilaration proved fragile – after the revolutionary wars and the Napoleonic experience, Europe settled down to the restored power of the old order. Ideas, however, do not always respect the political status quo. Though many of the Romantics turned conservative, seeking order and rest from turbulence, successive generations awoke to the realization of a new era in human affairs.

Carlyle mediated the enthusiasm of German literature for the philosophical idealism of Kant and his followers to a British audience. He found in the German writer, Jean Paul Friedrich Richter, a response to the new age which he could take to his own bosom. Carlyle translated these phrases from Richter's Preface to his novel *Hesperus*, and inserted them in his essay on the German:

But there will come another era . . . when it shall be light, and man will awaken from his lofty dreams, and find – his dreams still there, and that nothing is gone save his sleep . . .

Infinite Providence, Thou wilt cause the day to dawn. But as yet struggles the twelfth-hour of the Night; nocturnal birds of prey are on the wing, spectres uproar, the dead walk, the living dream.

Carlyle recalled the twelfth-hour image in his delineation of the present time of upheaval (the eighteen-thirties) in an essay of 1831:

Man has walked by the light of conflagrations, and amid the sound of falling cities; and now there is darkness, and long watching till it can be morning.

Through Carlyle, then, the image of the dark night of Richter, with its sense of suspension and waiting, passed on to the Victorian poets. In them we find the two main implications behind the idea: so in Matthew Arnold:

> Wandering between two worlds, one dead,
> The other powerless to be born,

and the well-known image of the darkling plain:

> Swept with confused alarms of struggle and flight,
> Where ignorant armies clash by night.

Thus for the failure of hope; but also in the later Arnold, we read:

> He breaks the winter of the past;
> A green, new earth appears.
> Millions, whose life in ice lay fast
> Have thoughts, and smiles, and tears.

The old order was passing away – ' "Your creeds are dead . . ./
Your social order too!" ' – but:

> The world's great order dawns in sheen,
> . . .
> Divinelier imaged, clearer seen,
> With happier zeal pursued.

A similar awareness is found in Tennyson, thus in 'Morte
D'Arthur':

> The old order changeth, yielding place to new,
> And God fulfils Himself in many ways,
> Lest one good custom should corrupt the world.

But still, it is weary waiting for the new world to come,

> . . . Come, my friends,
> 'Tis not too late to seek a newer world.

Society and men grow corrupt and brutish in the interim, then
returns the visionary certainty again:

> Ring out old shapes of foul disease;
>   Ring out the narrowing lust of gold;
>   Ring out the thousand wars of old,
> Ring in the thousand years of peace.
>
> Ring in the valiant man and free,
>   The larger heart, the kindlier hand;
>   Ring out the darkness of the land,
> Ring in the Christ that is to be.

And so in Charles Kingsley, J. A. Symonds, in other Victorian
poets too, not to speak of the revivalist hymns of the time (see
the old *Methodist Hymn Book*), the new age, with its associations
of new heaven and new earth, recurs.

But the days of buoyancy and exhilaration were numbered,
not merely for the individual artist but for the movement as a
whole. Conditions changed and the call that had been raised
was answered in a way almost the inverse of what the Romantic
prophets had expected.

With the dawn of the twentieth century the optimistic side of the new age waned, but the dark age, the world of blight and nothingness, the Victorian wasteland transfigured on a great scale, this feature has grown all too pervasively:

> This is the dead land
> This is the cactus land
> Here the stone images
> Are raised, here they receive
> The supplication of a dead man's hand
> Under the twinkle of a fading star.

Where Eliot sees only the death of a civilization, W. B. Yeats could see a palingenesia, a rebirth, an old civilization dying amidst blood and madness, and a new civilization beginning. History was a cyclical affair, and a civilization must move through a cycle, reach its full moon, wane, and collapse with hysterical violence:

> Things fall apart; the centre cannot hold;
> Mere anarchy is loosed upon the world,
> The blood-dimmed tide is loosed, and everywhere
> The ceremony of innocence is drowned.

At the same time a new God would be born, and in time take the place of the old. In the mean time, those who lived through the apocalyptic process of death and rebirth must display joy amidst all the tragedy:

> Hector is dead and there's a light in Troy;
> We that look on but laugh in tragic joy.

Yeats is considered the last of the Romantic poets and it is fitting that he should conclude the tradition of poetry stretching back to Shelley and Blake, both of whom he greatly admired. For with Yeats died the idea of the poet as seer, the man who could perform as a weathercock and discern the spiritual climate of the age.

What had been achieved, then, and why had it proved so fragile? In its prophetic function, Romanticism had not failed in its task of awakening Europe to the advent of a new order, in which political freedom would be established, and a new revelation of spiritual verity would sweep men's souls and deliver them up to the new millennium. The chill wind of the Enlightenment had succumbed (so one might have thought) to the soft but thrilling breezes of 'a new revelation of the godlike', as Carlyle expressed it. It was true that the old world had been destroyed by the French Revolution and the mockery of the *Philosophes* and that the new world was anxiously awaited. The Romantics had done their best to rise to the challenge of the new conditions and fill the spiritual vacuum. They moved souls with their verse, awakened men to the injustices of society, strove to inculcate high ideals such as the freedom of the nations within one universal commonwealth – so Mazzini – and the brotherhood of all races and creeds foreseen by Goethe and Schiller. They even aspired, as Beethoven, to make men gods. The darkness of man's infancy had passed and the dawning of his longed-for maturity had arrived, according to Fichte. The image of the phoenix arising from his ashes was beloved of the Saint-Simonians, and the golden age that some had said was in the past was really yet to come.

It was too wide a hope, too sincerely and profoundly voiced to be called the mere day-dream of a group of poets. This is proved by the persistence of the new age motif long after the great Romantics were dead. But they had not conceived of it in terms of coal production, railway travel and suspension bridges – though the engineering feats of Brunel had their own messianic character too.

What the last Romantics like John Ruskin appreciated was that the spiritual heart of the Romantic message had remained unanswered. Men had not been changed inwardly, were as far off as ever from the nurtured, striving individuals we find in *Wilhelm Meister*. Instead they had been won by easier means to more obvious riches. And the wealth they were creating was not even making for more beautiful cities or healthier people. But while the realms of philosophy and politics succumbed to materialism and the marshalling of force, the irreconcilable and explosive elements within a social order in flux threatened the emergence of a frightening age of transition. A new age to the foolish and the wise, observed Carlyle with irony in 1850, but not the new age he had hoped for twenty-five years before.

To Science and Materialism

In retrospect the Romantic dream of a new heaven and a new earth seemed doomed from the start: the nineteenth century was an age of material transformation, and so Marx and Engels were surely right to condemn the unscientific impracticality of the utopian dreamers of the first thirty years of the century. Romanticism was useful as a quarry from which one could cart off important ideas – as Marx and Engels plundered Saint-Simon – without the least tribute. The Romantics were impractical and based their speculations on no tangible reality, whereas their critics took their best ideas and grounded them in fact and science.

Yet for all that, Romanticism bequeathed to later nineteenth-century thought its fundamental insights. Hegel was the postscript of Kant, Schelling and Fichte; Marx and Engels derived their millennial conception of a historical process coming at last to fruition from the German idealists. No one denies it – yet the beneficiaries made short shrift of their benefactors. It is true that new developments in thought more often than not involve repudiation of the previous system from which the new movement has nevertheless learnt much. The Romantics repudiated the Enlightenment, but adopted the tolerance and love of freedom the earlier movement facilitated. But we might argue that Romanticism brought something of enduring significance which both the Enlightenment and the positivistic movements of the mid-nineteenth century lacked: this was the openness to the transcendental dimension and the refusal to limit human experience to what could be measured by the instruments of calculation alone.

The vital accompaniment to recognizing the existence of transcendent reality was the understanding that man could not change his world for the better without changing himself.

Positivistic schemes of action merely reverted to the eighteenth-century view that if social conditions were perfected, man would be made perfect. Romanticism insisted on the need to reform the individual, by appealing to his higher nature and by nourishing his soul. Not that it fought shy of collective activity: it was here that Romanticism stressed almost inevitably the primacy of the great man and hero. Messianic connotations were at the heart of Romantic views of history and society. Thomas Carlyle has been held responsible on the score of hero-worship, yet his ideas were no more than the explicit formulation of ideas implicit in Goethe, Fichte, Saint-Simon and Byron.

The Romantics were their own messiahs, but their theories admitted the possibility of the entrance of a universal Messiah. The greatest advances in history were facilitated by men who were morally, intellectually and spiritually superior to the men of their own time. Not ambition, Fichte insisted, but the pure devotion to truth, drove the hero to change the world by virtue of great deeds. It was not illusion and lies fathered by crude men hungry for power that the Romantics honoured – but men of honour and courage like Mazzini and Garibaldi. The dictators who came later were the creation of mass movements and mass cupidity – Louis Napoleon was a political opportunist and a true son of the new age of realism and materialism. Romanticism had espoused the elevation of mankind through faith in the great individual – here too it fell short in that great men, though nourished under its tutelage, were not transcendent enough. The materialists would diminish the ideal of the messiah, but the Romantic ideal erred only in its degree of faith: the universal Messiah could be greater even than imagined.

But here as in other things the change to naturalistic ways of thinking reduced and debarred ideas held by the Romantics. Very few men aspired to be heroes and this was the age of democracy. The old Romantic giants had no love for democracy when they lived to see it. In the new world of equality men would be redeemed by science – and science held no illusions about man the hero. It was in the cause of man the biped, devoid of transcendent hopes, that Huxley worsted the guardian of Victorian religious hope, the Bishop of Oxford.

By the 1860s the prevailing ideology reflected the ascendancy of science. Among intellectuals humanism, science and the idea of progress were the constituents of a new creed. The assumption was that these were the shaping factors of the modern world. Probably this was the moment when these concepts were at their most evangelical, as rationalist lecturers arose to repeat Huxley's victory and throw back the reactionary force of religion. In England and France earnest men and women strove to demonstrate that humanism might constitute the moral core of the new society. The residue of millenarianism helped bolster their certitude in the inexorable march of progress and the new evangel of moral agnosticism – religion stripped of its irrationality and barbarism, accommodated to a new world picture founded upon scientific evidence and the knowledge that miracles did not happen. In the humane, lofty rationality discernible in the writing of Ernest Renan and George Eliot, the new agnostic creed seemed to gain its apogee.

However, the base was very narrow. Ethical agnosticism did not nourish the growing urban proletariats of Europe – the more virulent strain of atheistic revolutionary socialism, as taught by Frederick Lassalle and his followers, was making headway in Germany. Cavour and Bismarck were breaking with any pretence of idealism that might hitherto have influenced European diplomacy. Bismarck could teach even the scientific socialists a thing or two about realistic strategy in the array of international and domestic political forces. Whether or not old protestations of honour had meant anything when a revolt was to be suppressed, the Bismarckian new era demonstrated in fact what the naturalists were insisting on in theory: the world was the arena of natural laws, where superior force would always be victorious. Blood, iron and sagacity united a nation – principles, resolutions and debates did not.

It was not, perhaps could not be, realized at the time what this open recognition of strength and force as the deciding factors in human affairs might portend for a world rapidly amassing larger and larger units of potential power. Nation would pit its strength against nation in a coming epoch. Now was the moment rather to open the coal seams, build the factories, establish power in central government and equip the armies of tomorrow.

Aftermath

It seems that relatively suddenly, by the beginning of the last quarter of the century, sensitive spirits awoke to the realization that something had gone wrong with the millennium. And these were pre-eminently the artists and philosophers whom the new world had elbowed out. It would be Nietzsche, a renegade romantic, who would denounce with the fullest power the nightmare world the late nineteenth-century artist found himself living in; but others who were less alienated would also endeavour to delineate its conflicts and contra-dictions.

The grandiose speculations of the mid-century did not lack emulation in the later generation, but the new men were already mouthing formulas. The middle men went about popularizing the wisdom of the previous decades unappreciative that it was already *passé*. The wisdom of the ethical society was adulterated and passed down to the artisan class in the form of republicanism and atheism. So too the millennialism of the earlier decades received greater circulation, and was taken into new causes like imperialism.

There were few cheers for the heroic redeemer now: men were to be saved through allegiance to collective groupings: the imperial service, the national political parties, leagues of different sorts, above all race and nation.

While corporation gave the common man a sense of security and identity, it threw the individual artist into a realm of isolation where his identity was in crisis. Loss of faith was now a fact of life, to be lived with, not bemoaned. But there was no exhilarating sense of freedom in agnosticism now. Artists huddled together in groups and small societies to stave off the threat of the outside world. They sought leadership in desperation, whilst at the same time unwilling to admit their nakedness. Some, like Yeats, sought the comfort of the great dead. Wilde projected a totally artificial mask: behind both was the awful sense of futility, fuelled by the feeling that everything had already been done. This belittling consciousness could turn to spite, as in Samuel Butler's attempts to pull down the idols of the past.

But the genius turned spite and hatred into a powerful condemnation of the whole century. Nietzsche hated above all the weakness of his own position, and so he denigrated the men who had preceded him on the path to alienation. But his greatest vitriol was reserved for ordinary men. They believed themselves so secure in the world they had created with the God they had created, but their world was founded on an illusion. God was dead – all the gods were dead and man was just a shadow.

Throughout the nineteenth century, from Goethe to Matthew Arnold, writers had taken man whole – flawed it is true, conditioned by society and religion – but nevertheless a specific identity. The Romantic view of man was that he was potentially a hero, that he was possessed of life and choice, with a soul and unlimited sensibilities. The naturalists saw men as social beings, ordinary not extraordinary, limited by time and place, but possessed of a fixed humanity. But by the end of the century there has been a profound change. It is not just that man becomes the helpless victim of social, economic and psychological complexities and no longer the controller of his environment; it is the moral centre, the consistent view of man as a single whole, that has broken down. The shift is seen in the writings of Ibsen, in the move away from the social dramas of his middle period, to the world of internal guilt, failure and crisis of identity of the late plays. The way was open to Freud to erode still further the idea that man is a rational being.

Thus the advance guard of the end of the century. European

civilization collectively stood unknowingly on the brink of conflagration, the messianic zeal of the first half-century now channelled into the nation states and the class politics that represented centres of mass power. The new age had yielded the new technology, but this had remained in the hands of the old morality. There was no overall allegiance to mankind as the Enlightenment sages and the Romantic visionaries had hoped. There was no higher morality either with the accession to power of the people. Instead there was rivalry, competing theories of social behaviour ready to appeal to force.

What had happened to the millennium? Where had the promise of the first decades of the century gone to? Did History really have a goal after all, or had men been flattering their own vanities, merely misleading themselves? What framework could philosophy devise now to make sense of the world and give men the confidence to live in it? Or, to the contrary, was man doomed to live in a world without values? The atheists were insisting that man alone was the architect of his destiny, but who could say where that would lead if he was the weak, divided creature that Nietzsche projected? Whence could come the superman? Perhaps, before mankind could enter the kingdom of heaven it was appointed to pass through the fires of Armageddon.

II

Millennia of the Past

Writing of the order of thought which surrounded the foundation of Christianity, Renan had the following to say of the concept of millennium:

The Jew . . . thanks to a kind of prophetic sense which renders the Semite at times marvellously apt to see the great lines of the future, has made history enter religion. Perhaps he owes a little of this spirit to Persia. Persia, from an ancient period, conceived the history of the world as a series of evolutions, over each of which a prophet presided.

Each prophet had his *hazar*, or reign of a thousand years (chialism), and from these successive ages, analogous to the Avatär of India, is composed the course of events which prepared the reign of Ormuzd. At the end of the time when the cycle of chialisms shall be exhausted, the complete paradise will come. Men then will live happy; the earth will be as one plain; there will be only one language, one law, and one government for all. But this advent will be preceded by terrible calamities. Dahak (the Satan of Persia) will break his chains and fall upon the world. Two prophets will come to console mankind, and to prepare the great advent. These ideas ran through the world, and penetrated even to Rome, where they inspired a cycle of prophetic poems, of which the fundamental ideas were the division of the history of humanity into periods, the succession of the gods corresponding to these periods – a complete renovation of the world, and the final advent of a golden age. The book of Daniel, the book of Enoch, and certain parts of the Sibylline books are the Jewish expression of the same theory. These thoughts were certainly far from being shared by all; they were only embraced at first by a few persons of lively imagination, who were inclined towards strange doctrines.[1]

For the development of Christianity, several of the ideas above have a special importance. The belief in an apocalyptic destruction of the earth and the establishment of the kingdom of heaven on it thereafter is the most significant. But the concept of peace became a more subtle element in traditional views of the advent of Christ. For it was held that at his first coming into the world, Christ brought a peace that was rather more spiritual than physical. This was to some extent a matter of expediency: the promises of Isaiah concerning the appearance of the Messiah suggested that peace would reign to the extent that the lion would lie down with the lamb. Clearly, there had to be a spiritual meaning behind such pronouncements, or the carping of the Jews – who insisted that nothing at all had occurred with the appearance of Jesus of Nazareth – might seem justified. Thus the evangelist Luke has the multitude of the heavenly host say: 'Glory to God in the highest, and on earth peace among men with whom he is pleased' (II. xiv)

1. Ernest Renan, *The Life of Jesus*, pp. 48–9.

We find that John Milton, in his ode 'On the Morning of Christ's Nativity', has identified this spiritual peace with the actual conditions of the world at the time of the birth of Jesus, thus:

> No war or battle's sound
> Was heard the world around (ll. 53–4)

Renan takes a universal view, incorporating poets, religious expectancy and political conditions, in his picture of the world on the eve of the birth of Christianity:

In the degree that power became secularised, and passed into the hands of unbelievers, the Jewish people lived less and less for the earth, and became more and more absorbed by the strange fermentation which was operating in their midst. The world, distracted by other spectacles, had little knowledge of that which passed in this forgotten corner of the East. The minds abreast of their age were, however, better informed. The tender and clear-sighted Virgil seems to answer, as by a secret echo, to the second Isaiah. The birth of a child throws him into dreams of a universal palingenesis. These dreams were of every-day occurrence, and shaped into a kind of literature which was designated Sibylline. The quite recent formation of the empire exalted the imagination; the great era of peace on which it entered, and that impression of melancholy sensibility which the mind experiences after long periods of revolution, gave birth on all sides to unlimited hopes.[2]

Renan was surely right to include these various elements, for while modern historians are sceptical of cause and effect, the wellsprings of history are often mysterious. We still seek far for the precise cause of the French Revolution, if one cause there were, but Carlyle saw the force of change in history as deep and inscrutable:

. . . as was once written, 'though our clock strikes when there is a change from hour to hour, no hammer in the Horologe of Time peals through the Universe to proclaim that there is a change from era to era'. The true Beginning is oftenest unnoticed and unnoticeable. Thus do men go wrong in their reckoning; and grope hither and thither, not knowing where they are, in what course their history runs.[3]

2. op. cit. p. 34.
3. Thomas Carlyle, *Critical and Miscellaneous Essays*, vol. IV, p. 46.

Expectancy of the return of Christ among the Christians has risen and subsided on a number of occasions in history, though Christ himself denied knowledge of the day and hour. The apostolic Christian community lived in continual expectation of his imminent return. But by the end of the second century the apostolic age, with its spiritual gifts of 'ecstasy' and prophecy, was passing in favour of the period of organization and consolidation in the church. The first millennium after Christ would witness a revival of adventism, and again during the upheavals of the Reformation, until the later eighteenth century saw revivalism develop into a widespread readiness for the end of the world, the day of judgement and return of the Lord with his saints.

Each return of the millennial consciousness was accompanied – or itself depended on – changes in the political and social order of the time. Yet great as was the alteration of affairs in the sixteenth and seventeenth centuries in Europe, it compares but little with the era of the French Revolution and its aftermath. One strange congruence between the two periods is seen in the early nineteenth century Scottish preacher, Edward Irving, founder of the Irvingites, and one of the prophets of the end of the world and Second Coming. Irving revived the rhetorical style of preaching of his seventeenth-century Puritan ancestors, a gesture of Romanticism, and adopted the gift of tongues as the hallmark of his new apostolic community. The tragic career and early death of Irving, combined with his personal attractions (he was at one time the fashionable preacher of London society) adds to our awareness of his place in the Romantic age. But during the Reform crisis of 1830–32 sober churchmen and politicians like Dr Arnold and Robert Peel were half-inclined to accept Irving's millennial theories. Arnold too read in the signs of the times the end of a great age for the human race. The religious extremist Spencer Perceval actually succeeded in moving in the House of Commons for a general fast, and royalty, lords and commoners attended services on a national day of penance in March 1832.

These responses to an awareness of profound crisis and

change say something different about the millennial atmosphere of the nineteenth century as opposed to that of the first century AD. The birth of Christianity occurred during an age of optimism and peace in the Roman Empire; the nineteenth-century expectancy in Europe was born amidst fears of revolution and anarchy. And when prosperity and relative social quiet descended in England for a brief period in the mid-Victorian era, millennialism regained its benign character. Material well-being could always convince men for a time that all was for the best in the best of all possible worlds.

Here we return to the diversity of outlook which nevertheless is united by the millennial complexion of the first fifty years of the nineteenth century. The established of the land were rocked by fears of unrest from below – and the history of the century shows that most of the upper classes of Europe were not, like those in Britain, fortunate enough to sustain their position. Reformers were avid for change, and saw in the new age the fruition of their particular planned destiny for mankind. These saw hope of a material kind, but were eloquent in idealism. At the other extreme were the literalist religious sects who saw in the change the certain 'signs of the end'. Unlike the early Christians who read Isaiah almost with a symbolist almanac, the nineteenth-century adventists saw little symbolism in the scriptures – only dire threats of physical destruction and miraculous transformations of the material earth in mutations totally opposed to the laws of science. Yet they were precise enough when it came to setting dates for the Lord's return from the Books of Daniel, Isaiah and the other prophets – 1836, 1843–4 and 1866 were three variations arrived at. 'Sometimes the manner, the place, and the very day of the Second Advent were determined by calculations of the pious; and on one notorious occasion a concourse of votaries assembled at a designated spot to watch the clouds from which before nightfall a white-robed Messiah was to descend to earth.'[4]

So patently absurd are such manifestations of millennialism to the modern mind that it is easy to underestimate the impact

4. George Townshend, *The Promise of All Ages*, p. 112.

of the new age on thinking people of the last century. Yet it would be as foolish to dismiss the phenomenon because of the excesses of watchers after visible signs in the heavens as it would be to join them. The true beginning is often unnoticed and unnoticeable – yet it too has its invisible and visible signs. The historical evidence of an age is the visible sign to later generations that great changes are taking place. The millennialism of the first fifty years of the nineteenth century is a visible sign that something was happening. Perhaps there were also actual events transpiring in that time which it would take the light of later centuries to make manifest to all – even as the birth of a transforming faith in Palestine in 30 AD. took several centuries to be noticed by the world.

A New Religion

The nineteenth century was not lacking in new 'religions' designed to fulfil the needs of the new time. Saint-Simon came to the conclusion that technocratic ordering of society was not enough – men required an extra dimension which would bind together the various orders of society as Christianity was reputed to have done for the Middle Ages. Thus he conceived of a *nouveau Christianisme* which was to channel the perennial spirit of religion into the new social moulds of the nineteenth-century age of science. The other utopian socialists, Etienne Cabet and Charles Fourier, also conceived of their redemptive communities in almost religious terms. The bizarre forms of behaviour of these early socialist groups, with their development of arbitrary rites and acts of devotion directed toward the persons of their increasingly charismatic leaders, were scorned by Marx and Engels. Yet for all their excesses and inevitable collapse in the wake of personal feuds and obscurations, these communities did suggest that man was not to be redeemed by logic and machinery alone.

These secular faiths went alongside the utopian philosophies that had branched out of the eighteenth century. William Godwin and Mary Wollstonecraft made out of equality and female emancipation a creed, but their dry rationality belied the revolutionary changes such principles implied for the human psyche. It is not difficult to appreciate the suspicion with which these sects were regarded by the bourgeoisie, who were not altogether inaccurate in charging new attempts at social reconstruction as leading to the dissolution of marriage, the communal holding of women, atheism and social revolution. Throughout the nineteenth century the creation of a new religion held these connotations of lapse into indecency and immorality.

Yet the fact was that Europe and North America were subject to a turmoil of change in social relations hitherto defined by orthodox religious creeds. The hegemony of one particular form of religion in any given locality was every-where under siege. Unitarianism had crossed the Atlantic at the close of the eighteenth century and won a trickle of converts among the aristocracy and manufacturing classes. The new century, with its social rootlessness and mobility, witnessed the importation of more popular creeds like Mormonism and Christian Science from America. New evangelical sects proliferated, often established on the idea that they were the elect and were being prepared by the Lord for his imminent return.

By the middle of the century new religions were everywhere in evidence, and still appearing. Comtism, deriving from both the Romantic devotionalism of the Saint-Simonians and the cold logic of utilitarianism, turned the attention of the intellectual world to Paris. Religion and Science were reputedly joined together by the manifestly synthetic stratagems of Auguste Comte, who wanted men to worship the human race as divinity, and replace the saints with great men in history. Marxism itself had made a significant appearance on the eve of the 1848 revolutions. Opening with the new message that 'the history of all hitherto existing society is the history of class struggle', and ending with the invocation 'Working men of all countries unite', *The Communist Manifesto* laid its claims to the minds and hearts of the human race.

Perhaps the most remarkable feature of this ferment of spiritual change is that which generally goes unremarked by historians: hardly anyone has observed that the great religious renaissances of the world's history occur not in the Western world, but take place in the East. It seems partly intriguing and at the same time partly incongruent that we speak of a new religion like Mormonism arising in the United States – for when has a universal faith ever emerged from that country, or even Europe? The whole significance of nineteenth-century millennialism cannot be construed until we turn to the East and verify the position there.

The picture, with one vital exception, is disappointing. The Eastern world of the early nineteenth century sleeps in the lethargy of hundreds – even thousands – of years of orthodoxy.

The Islamic world, it is true, was experiencing yet the effects of the Wahhabi movement and its mission to purify Islam. The change would indeed be an important one for Muslim practice in the next century and longer. But the movement was essentially backward-looking in its reference back to the pure Islam of the apostolic age. Hinduism was witnessing the reforms of the Brahmo Samaj, but as Professor Zaehner points out 'its inspiration was Western'.[5] The millennialism of the evangelical Christian sects in the West had almost wholly passed by the Greek Orthodox Church as it had the Roman Catholic. Overall the impression we get of the East in the early nineteenth century is of a very considerably quieter, almost atrophied culture, compared to the West. But there was one exception, the Bábí movement in Persia which first had its impact in the 1840s, and later gained the attention of several very able Europeans.

This movement was from the first messianic in character. The majority of its leading apostles were from the Shaykhí sect of Shí'i Islam, formed by Shaykh Aḥmad of Aḥsá, an Arab who had achieved eminence and later some notoriety in the Persia of Fatḥ-'Alí Sháh. Shaykh Aḥmad had fallen out with some of the leading mujtahids or doctors of the Shí'i

5. R. C. Zaehner, *Hinduism*, Oxford, 1966, p. 150.

community, partly over doctrine, and partly over personality. Under his successor, Siyyid Kázim of Rasht, the Shaykhís were a distinct school, heterodox to the majority of the Shí'a, and more active than the body of their fellow Muslims in seeking out the source of charismatic renewal promised in Islam.

It was from the ranks of Shaykhism that Siyyid 'Alí-Muḥammad of Shiraz, known to history as the Báb, forged a movement that in a few brief years convulsed Persia and attracted the attention of the European Powers. The Báb declared himself to be the promised one foretold by Siyyid Kázim, the one who would renew the faith of Islam. He made the pilgrimage to Mecca, and there made his announcement to a number of pilgrims, as well as to the Sherif of Mecca. Before leaving Persia, the Báb encouraged his followers to spread the news of his appearance throughout the nation, and sent missionaries to Iraq and India. He promised to appear among his followers in the holy city of Kerbila in Iraq, but subsequently changed his plans and returned to his native Shiraz. His merchant family did not support his claims, but his uncle and guardian endeavoured to protect him from the inevitable onslaught of the clergy soon to explode.

The Báb was soon placed under house arrest, and later imprisoned. The remarkable fact about his short career as prophet and religious leader is that most of it was spent in the seclusion of his uncle's house, then elsewhere under house arrest and, for the last four years, before his execution in 1850, in prison. Yet such was his influence that he generated a major upheaval in the state, and galvanized his followers, who were led by his mainly youthful deputies, to deeds of reckless bravery. The Bábís fought resolutely against enemies of far greater numbers, and included women and children in their ranks. They were treacherously betrayed on several occasions by the false promises of their assailants, and succumbed to horrific massacres that, however, still could not quench the ardour of those who remained.

The Báb's followers went into battle with the black standard unfurled – denoting the presence of the expected one of Islam.

They fought, on the whole, not to threaten the existing powers, but to vindicate the claims of their leader, claims that were religious in essence. However, the close intertwining of religion and state in Muslim countries ensured oppression by government and clergy together, although a significant number of Bábí converts came from the clergy themselves.

Although recent writers have stressed the political complexion of the Bábí movement, it is still true that the main reason for its violent reception in Persia was its religious innovation. The Báb was not just the custodian of the Shí'i Imams, or the renewer of the spirit of Islam: short as his career was, and bloody though the persecution of his followers turned out to be after his death, in the pogrom of 1852, he was the creator of an independent religion, with its own scripture and laws, and a separate claim to divine inspiration, rather than, as in the case of Mormonism and Christian Science, a supplementary one.

The impact of the Bábí movement in Iran was first apprehended by Europeans as a stirring within the hopelessly corrupt and decadent social order of an effete Islamic state. Persia, like Turkey, was a sick man, but its sickness did not impinge upon Europe, and its importance as a barrier to Russian expansion into India was not yet so great in the eyes of the British. The Bábí cause was seen alternately as a socialistic movement and another example of oriental occultism and mysticism.[6] Yet the figure of the Báb held a romance-value for the more sensitive. Later in the century Sarah Bernhardt wanted to act in a play about him; for the idealistic, the Báb fitted into the mode of nineteenth-century messianic figures who sacrificed their lives for liberty and freedom. Perhaps too the tragic circumstances surrounding his short life and martyrdom touched the chords of a Christian culture.

Thus the Bábí movement gained publicity in the West almost from its inception, but, as we have seen with other 'new religions', European commentators were quick to associate it with communism and wife-sharing. But in the writings of two

6. See M. Momen, *The Bábí and Bahá'í Religions, 1844–1944*, section A, *passim*.

French littérateurs, the Comte de Gobineau and A.-L.-M. Nicolas, the person of the Prophet of Shiraz, as the Báb came to be known, received treatment that amounted to veneration, even acknowledgement of his creed. A.-L.-M. Nicolas translated the *Bayán*, the Bible of the Bábís, into French. Gobineau eulogized the Persian prophet in *Les Religions et les Philosophes dans l'Asie Centrale*, and partly as a result of these efforts the Báb became known to a quite wide circle of the intelligentsia of Europe, including Matthew Arnold who introduced the Báb in an essay on the Shí'a entitled *A Persian Passion Play*. As a noble, lost cause, the religion of the Báb was known in Europe, and the enchanting, Christ-like character of its founder inspired plays and essays.

However, the cynosure of the new movement is not to be associated with the Báb himself, and its development must not be considered to be ended by the Báb's death. The Persian prophet's teaching centred on the appearance of another prophet far greater than himself; his mission would be to inaugurate a new cycle in the destiny of mankind which would last hundreds of thousands of years. In this respect the promise of the Báb recalls the prophecy of the ancient Persian religion mentioned by Renan: Zoroastrianism, the faith supplanted in Persia by Islam, insisted on the establishment of a state of paradise on earth after convulsions had destroyed the old cycle of human affairs. Within thirteen years of the death of the Báb his faith was transformed by a second messianic figure, justifying his station by the Báb's reference to the great one who should follow him, and the scriptures of the world's past religions which he adduced were replete with prophecies of a universal Messiah who would appear at the time of the end and reorganize the affairs of the whole planet. This second Messiah was Ḥusayn 'Alí of Tehran, known to history as Bahá'u'lláh, 'the Glory of God'. The overwhelming proportion of Bábís followed Bahá'u'lláh and were called Bahá'ís.

The Bahá'í Faith and the New Age

The mission of Bahá'u'lláh lasted nearly forty years – from 1853 to 1892, during which time the Bahá'í Faith emerged from Persia and, owing to the banishment of its head, removed to the vicinity of Akka in Syria. Bahá'u'lláh became renowned throughout the Middle East, and won adherents from the Jewish, Christian, Muslim and Zoroastrian religions. Towards the end of his life he received the only European who in his own capacity took an interest in the Bahá'í cause – E. G. Browne, the Cambridge orientalist. Browne had already shown great interest in the Báb, but was misled by the half-brother of Bahá'u'lláh, Subh-i-Azal, who misused his position as appointed custodian of the Bábí community to spread lies and deceit about Bahá'u'lláh. Though Browne could perceive the influence Bahá'u'lláh had come to wield over the Báb's erstwhile followers, and testified to the striking importance of his teaching, he failed to disentangle himself from the machinations of the Azalís. The result was that the Bahá'í Faith was represented to the Western world as a schismatic development of the Bábí movement, instead of what it patently was: its renewal, revitalization and fulfilment.

The consequences of this can be overestimated, but there is no doubt that it played its part in the meagre coverage the Bahá'í movement received in Europe during the lifetime of Bahá'u'lláh, as against the publicity received by the Báb. Other factors were the exile and imprisonment of Bahá'u'lláh for most of the forty years of his ministry, and the generally passive posture of his followers in the face of the combined persecution of the Persian and Ottoman Turkish governments.

Despite this, the Bahá'í Faith is to be seen as a truly remarkable product of the nineteenth century, for in its doctrines we find a complete, perhaps perfect, representation of the highest aspirations of the new age.

A broad principle of the Bahá'í Faith – in fact its main focus in terms of importance – was that of the unity of mankind. The most idealistic formulation of enlightenment and post-enlightenment philosophers such as Kant, the belief in a universal commonwealth of nations was propounded in Palestine in an impregnable prison-citadel by this extraordinary Persian, Bahá'u'lláh. The foresight of such an appeal was readily appreciated by E. G. Browne who recorded the following words of Bahá'u'lláh during their interview in 1890: 'We desire but the good of the world and the happiness of the nations. That all nations should become one in faith and all men as brothers; that the bonds of affection and unity between the sons of men should be strengthened.' It was already becoming accepted by this time that Bahá'u'lláh had demonstrated his love for this principle by the years of banishment and detention he had suffered on its account. He told Browne further: 'yet they deem Us a stirrer-up of strife and sedition worthy of bondage and banishment'. Certainly at that time there were existing no two governments and peoples less likely to adopt such an ideal as the unity of mankind than Persia and Turkey. Nor can we find, perusing the advocates of Sunni and Shí'i Islam, any comparable belief in the writings of Persians and Turks of this period. Bahá'u'lláh stood in the vanguard of philosophy, alongside the most revered European philosophers, but as he knew no European language and had received little formal education, the utterances of Bahá'u'lláh carry that much greater force.

Again, as a nation once renowned for its poets and general literacy among the learned, Persia had sunk to a miserable level in the nineteenth century. Its only cadre of educated were the *mullas* – men intent upon maintaining their hold over an ignorant populace and a shifting and incompetent monarchy. Bahá'u'lláh countered such irresponsibility by insisting on universal educational opportunities, the abolition of priesthood, and the duty of every mature adult of sane mind to search out truth independently for himself. This last exhortation was to be considered a religious obligation. No such teaching was to be found in the accepted orthodoxy of any existing world faith at that time. Had such a principle existed there would have been no need for the contests between churchmen and free-thinkers that would eventually lead to the defection of the intelligentsia from religion, and through them the masses. Moreover, the principle of independent investigation of truth was at the core of the Western liberal frame of mind. Needless to say, Bahá'u'lláh had not read John Stuart Mill.

Bahá'u'lláh's writings in fact put the highest emphasis on the need to abandon prejudicial modes of thought, founded on no better criterion than centuries of obscurantism. The bars to progress are exactly those hidebound traditions which have no basis in illuminated thought but rather have developed from superstition and the selfish interests of erstwhile leaders. The people have always been debarred from the pure truth of religion by its *soi-disant* initiates, the priests and doctors. But in spite of these trenchant criticisms of clergy, some of the most eminent early converts to the new faith were previously high ranking clerics.

Moreover, whilst Bahá'í teaching inculcates respect and acceptance of government authority, it makes clear judgements on the necessary basis for government. In a letter to Queen Victoria Bahá'u'lláh praised the monarch for taking counsel with representatives of her people. Elsewhere he wrote that a combination of monarchical and republican government was most beneficial – implying that the two principles of hereditary leadership and democratic consultation were to be harmonized. The British constitution of this time was probably the closest to such an ideal and therefore received Bahá'u'lláh's commendation. But the crowned heads of Europe as a whole were severely reproved for increasing daily expenditure on ceremonial and armies and placing the burden upon the backs of the poor. In the 1870s Bahá'u'lláh assured the monarchs of Germany, Austria-Hungary and Imperial Russia that their militarism could only lead to the collapse of their thrones. Already, Louis Napoleon had succumbed to the militarist's nemesis – and had been warned of his fate by the Persian prisoner-exile the year before it occurred.

Perhaps the most forward-looking aspect of Bahá'u'lláh's counsels to the great powers of Europe was his delineation of a course for collective disarmament involving the convening of a congress to which representatives of each nation would be sent possessing the mandatory power of their governments to negotiate. But not even this machinery would be enough to create a lasting world peace – what was required above all was the spirit among all men to carry it out. Here Bahá'u'lláh was sadly far in advance of his time: his admonitions were ignored, and the first great assembly of nations was only convened after the World War that ended in 1918. Nor was the conference of Versailles of 1919 – replete as it was with acrimony and vindictiveness – remotely capable of establishing collective security for mankind. This fateful failure of the leaders of the world had terrible implications for generations yet unborn. Bahá'u'lláh acknowledged that as mankind had turned its back upon the way to peace it must traverse the deep gulfs of upheaval, war and social chaos before it could emerge chastened by the experience.

For not only in the matter of international order but also in that of the cohesion of each individual state, the principles of the new age were not being implemented. Long before the Charter of Human Rights, Bahá'u'lláh voiced the necessity for freedom of worship and belief, the equality of all men before the law, the abolition of extremes of wealth and poverty and the acceptance by the state of its responsibility for the care and material and spiritual well-being of its citizens. One by one these principles would be adopted by mankind – yet they are to be found in their entirety in the writings of Bahá'u'lláh. By any standards it was a remarkable programme, standing associated with the best ideas to be found within European philosophy as a whole. The nineteenth century was able to accept them – the human race was on the verge of its coming of age. Yet the nineteenth century did not adopt them and thus the course of modern history was irredeemably set.

At this point it is necessary to view the claims of the founder of the Bahá'í Faith – for comprehensive as the principles were which he enunciated, it is not merely as a philosopher-sage that he addressed himself to mankind. Bahá'u'lláh ubiquitously in his writings referred to the revelationary character of both his knowledge and his effect over those around him. After 1863 he was unequivocal in associating himself with the voice of divinity and his mission with the direct will of that inspirational force. Theologically, the founder of no previous religion is as forthright and undeviating in his conception of his own station and role in human affairs. 'O king!' he wrote to the Shah of Persia, 'I was but a man like others, asleep upon My couch, when lo, the breezes of the All-Glorious were wafted over Me, and taught me the knowledge of all that hath been. This thing is not from Me, but One Who is Almighty and All-Knowing.' Viewed together with the wisdom already set out, it is a remarkable claim and all the more overpowering when we consider these words addressed to the kings of the earth collectively in Bahá'u'lláh's most holy book, the *Kitáb-i-Aqdas*: 'Ye are but vassals, O Kings of the earth! He Who is the King of kings hath appeared, arrayed in His most wondrous glory, and is summoning you unto Himself . . .' The megalomaniac does not address himself to an absolute monarch – and withal his gaoler – as Bahá'u'lláh to Sultan 'Abdu'l-Azíz, in the tone of admonisher, if he wishes to advance his position. Yet neither was the act suicidal, for Bahá'u'lláh outlived the Sultan whose guilt led to his own assassination in 1876, gained his freedom from the confines of Akka and died surrounded with honour in the mansion of Bahjí in 1892. Then a telegram was sent to another Sultan, 'Abdu'l-Ḥamíd, with the simple words: 'The Sun of Bahá has set.' The exile and prisoner had that stature which no prison could contain.

However we view the religious genius of Bahá'u'lláh, the scope of his teaching, the testimony of his endurance and the persistence of his influence from that time onward must lead us to draw parallels with the birth of the other major religions of the world. The Bahá'í Faith has its place in an era of millennialism and a century of the profoundest change in human history. Religions are born at the turning points of history, yet we can only say this with hindsight, for invariably the birth of a new spirit goes undetected in the world and an age, sometimes ages, pass before it is recognized. The Bahá'í Faith has that intimate relationship with the nineteenth century which it is not yet possible to appreciate fully. For as an expanding movement still youthful and perhaps centuries from its zenith, it defies us now to fix its perspective.

Likewise the person of Bahá'u'lláh remains inscrutable: during the mature years of his life he suffered banishment, imprisonment, and finally nominal detention. Yet in that time he was able to write or dictate the equivalent of one hundred volumes – which few Westerners today can claim to have read in their entirety, the majority remaining in their Persian and Arabic originals, untranslated. The early pioneer of comparative religion, Dr Cheyne, wrote thus of his reputation: 'There was living quite lately a human being of such consummate excellence that many think it both permissible and inevitable even to identify him mystically with the invisible Godhead.'[7] Certainly Bahá'u'lláh had in abundance what modern writers like to call 'charisma'. The Bahá'í Faith has spread, and that is his most important monument. Wherever his followers are found today, the spirit of the new age enunciated by their Master continues to grow and become enriched.

Retrospect

It is the job of the historian to illuminate the past, not to prophesy the future. He may illustrate a line of thought, but not insist on the conclusiveness of his theories, for history is its own brand of science and may only present collocations of evidence in various forms, to be weighed, evaluated, and judged upon by others.

I have suggested that a millennial spirit motivated or influenced many different kinds of Europeans in the years following on the French Revolution, and that this developed well into the first half of the new century. An expectancy was generated which held political, social, religious and material

7. Quoted in Townshend, *Promise*, p. 17.

connotations. Its highest cultural expression is to be found in the great Romantic figures, and these in turn bequeathed to later generations formative ideas brought forth under the influence of the idea of the new age. Later, however, as the century grew older, the *élan* which motivated the early prophets of Romanticism receded. Inspiration, as critics of Victorian literature inform us, gave way to 'practicality'; ideals were replaced by 'realistic' attitudes. The foundations of the racial and class conflicts of the near future were laid. Imperialism gained a deeper root in the world, and loyalties to the ideals of peace, unity and brotherhood waned. On the other hand, the advance of science laid the foundations for material development.

If we were plotting a chart of the cultural richness and height of hope of the previous two centuries, we might see it begin to rise at about the middle of the eighteenth century, go into a steep elevation during the years 1790 to 1830, level out somewhat thereafter till 1870, then enter a decline. Although the idea of the millennium became general in the second half of the nineteenth century, it lost its edge so far as writers and intellectuals were concerned, but became staid and popular, the battle cry of liberal papers and thereafter imperialists and popular socialists. The War of 1914–18 dealt the idea of progress a telling blow from which it never recovered, except during moments of superficial prosperity.

What then did happen to the millennium? Was it merely an incidental change in the barometer of history – something explained away in contingent terms, without any more fundamental impulse? If we take such a view we make the implicit judgement that history has no rhyme or reason. If we take a 'scientific', Marxist view (and one that is very much heir to nineteenth-century frameworks of thought) we might hold that a great change in human society did take place, but one that has hardly been completed yet: the stage of socialist revolution. The liberal view of history has now more or less died, attached as it was to the idea of peaceful progress towards parliamentary democracy and free institutions. The arena of carnage in the twentieth century dealt its death blows.

If we turn to the view of history that emerges from the Bahá'í movement as it has developed from the time of its founder, another evaluation of modern history emerges. I intend to investigate that view in another essay, but this much can be said as summary of our theme. The Bahá'í Faith presents a hypothesis which can be taken with the historical evidence or rejected. This view holds that the expectancy and hope generated during the period in question meant two things above all: first, mankind had reached a new stage in its development, that of the coming of age or maturity of mankind which philosophers like Lessing and Fichte articulated. But secondly, the key to our understanding of this new time rests on our recognition that a universal Messiah was due at exactly the same moment. He would bring a new spiritual springtime that would in time father a great civilization. The Messiah is the key to the historical process – without him evolution would be painfully slow. The Romantic veneration of the hero as the *leitmotif* within history is amplified in the Bahá'í belief that great Figures who appear from millennium to millennium reveal God to man, and expedite his path to perfection. Such ideas were also implicit in Hinduism and Zoroastrianism, as we have seen – the theory is brought up to date and exemplified in the actual foundation of the Bahá'í Faith.

The millennium is thus fulfilled in Bahá'í belief with the appearance of the Báb and Bahá'u'lláh – and their coming fulfils the expectancy of the major religious traditions of mankind. The lost hope of the nineteenth century is its failure to recognize its Messiah, and its ignoring of his summons to peace and unity. The trough that then ensues in human history is extremely perilous. It is characterized by atheism and a more general loss of purpose and belief amongst all peoples. Without a satisfactory world picture human society cannot long remain cohesive. The old paths no longer help, they hinder instead. Man as the author of his own destiny is a sorry creature. Nations of men supported by no divine idea and led by inane leaders lose their way and head for the ditch. Collectively, the human race faces the unloosing of satan and blackest night. The way out leads through Armageddon. Only in the ancient promise of the world's religions can mankind regain its faith in the future. Ultimately, only in recognizing the fulfilment of that promise can the promise itself be redeemed, and the yearned-for kingdom of heaven be realized.

From Vision to Nightmare

> What prevents men from uniting as brothers is their
> own base inadequacy. Slaves cannot unite; cowards
> cannot unite; the ignorant cannot unite. It is only by
> obeying our highest impulses that we can unite.
>
> *Henry Miller*

IN AN AGE of disintegration prophets and soothsayers abound; men run hither and thither after knowledge, but rarely attain it. When a state of disequilibrium prevails, those who proffer diagnoses are eagerly embraced by the chronically insecure who, if they cannot acquire certitude, are at least athirst to know the reasons for their illness. Hence in our own times the vogue for all manner of pseudo-savants – from devisers of religious cults to journalists and broadcasters. No man can escape the sickness of his age, and indeed it is the man of thought who is most likely to contract it – for most human beings live according to formulas of action and belief that the intellectual vanguard have long since discarded.

The serious literature in such a period cannot eschew the curse of diagnosis and analysis. The conscious mind devours itself, but neither may the single, intuitive genius refound perception in its wholeness. Literature must portray man and his society in a state of restlessness, prey to all the strange diseases of modern life. Such a literature cannot be large in its achievement, may not even be tragic – for details oft repeated in life itself, in literature lose their strangeness and grandeur; and insanity, breakdown of relationships, desultoriness and dissolution cease to move us when we can read of them in any modern novel, as well as the daily newspaper, not to speak of experiencing them in actual life.

There may be but one outstanding literary genius in a century of self-dissection and neurosis – and arguably Franz Kafka was he. He was the original man who knew intuitively the impact of the modern age on the inner life. Hardly any other writer follows Kafka into the interior realms where the individual psyche registers the bewilderment of twentieth-century man before the terrors his society has to present him.

Yet Kafka was no social commentator in any collective sense: he sees only the individual. Other twentieth-century writers have endeavoured to make sense of the outer world, where answers can be sought in the less private realms of political, economic and social analysis. It is true that a powerful tradition already existed in the English language, represented by the giants of the nineteenth century, now largely discredited, which was more or less apolitical and outspoken in its condemnation of the modern world. But a new age, a new century, likes to believe itself independent of the thought of its grandsires. Prophets like Blake, Carlyle, Ruskin, Morris and their modern heirs as visionaries – figures like Yeats and Henry Miller – would be judged irrational, called hysterical, and dismissed as arcane. In their place arose new savants with renewed optimism. Idealism – not in its pure philosophical sense, for the new idealists were rationalists and, in the case of Wells, neo-Mechanist – emerged once more in the early twentieth century, as the Bernard Shaws, the H. G. Wellses, the Bertrand Russells took up once again the Godwinian vision of an egalitarian utopia.

It might have been partially true that the aged Ruskin turned to social radicalism from his inherited Toryism because his aesthetic senses were affronted by the smell of Victorian drainage. H. G. Wells would have exhorted him to optimism, to the glory of the coming utopia of clean pavements, electric lighting, and modern sanitation. Shaw would have invited him to cheer up and invest in the latest weaponry on behalf of the poor. The Romantic rejection of the machine was utterly old-fashioned, when everyone could see that machines were the salvation of mankind, the agency whereby the exploiting capitalist classes would be swept away as an anachronism. In the first three decades of the twentieth century scarcely anyone saw that the battle confronting man did not resolve itself into a struggle for the immense resources made available to humanity by the new technology. Indiscriminately, semi-consciously, all sides in the battleground of ideas, whether capitalist or communist, totalitarian or democrat, politician or ideologue, had come to accept the materialist mentality, the primacy of tangible, computable matter above the Imagination and Spirit. Then individuals began to realize, from the experience of their own minds and senses, that utopia-road was being paved with the tombstones of the dead multitudes laid by the hands of spiritual zombies. The world of the novels of such writers as George Orwell and Arthur Koestler, men whose imagination would not otherwise have risen much above the novelist's mean, now acquired something of the nightmare quality of Kafka himself. The political novel, which in Disraeli's hands had dealt with the outer world without much recourse to the workings of inner mind and soul, now emerged to lay bare an environment of terror; while the social satire, deftly wielded by the young Aldous Huxley in *Brave New World*, and by Evelyn Waugh, became the means of delineating a course of spiritual bankruptcy not beyond the achievement of twentieth-century hedonistic materialism.

In George Orwell's writings we see a politically committed mind of above average sensibility wrestling with the moral dilemmas of an era in which ethics have all but disappeared in the wake of political cupidity and duplicity. Orwell's stance is from the outset peculiar, due to his precise political commit-ment; he was essentially a moralist in the British tradition, but his open advocacy of left-wing politics held him all the while to a sectarian position his moral vision belied. That Orwell had not the gifts of a great imaginative writer most would agree from the evidence of his early novels. His adoption of the persona of the ordinary man, in *Keep the Aspidistra Flying* and

Coming Up for Air, was of a kind both with his socialism and his direct honesty. The directness of his moral vision, the total absence of cleverness, and the common man's suspicion of the flamboyant, make Orwell a disarming, almost naïve writer – though he covered any suggestion of *naïveté* by his adamant refusal to accept anything credulously, and that capacity to see through lies and subterfuge which the intense, scrupulous individual usually has.

Orwell was as a writer preoccupied with change; he saw the quiet, rural England of the previous century fast disappearing, and he saw cheap, commercial values replacing the native integrity and fair play which as a patriot he recognized in the English character. Orwell knew this to be the effect of a tremendous wave of change moving through world society as a whole, and though his books invariably display a strongly localized English character, their address often is far wider. 'Manor Farm' emerges from its setting in his beloved English countryside to take on the allegorical function as the homeland of the first socialist revolution. *Nineteen Eighty-Four* is set in the shabby England immediately post-Second World War, but it is soon distilled into a general environment of terror, recognizable to victims of totalitarianism the world over.

Orwell's awareness of change did not lead him to nostalgic indulgence alone; his peculiar grasp of social detail led him to observe the alteration in society's moral and behavioural code through such materials as picture postcards, crime stories in fiction and murder stories in the cheap Sunday press. When it came to political standards, no writer was so alive to the decline of thought and expression as evinced by the political literature of the period. In an unassuming manner Orwell was a master of language, and he could expose mercilessly the sham behind the language of even his own political creed. He was the scourge of totalitarian propaganda, and through his invention of terms like 'newspeak' and 'Big Brother' gave some life to the ailing democracies through his lurid warning of the spreading tyranny of centralized power. In the last analysis Orwell was a pessimist; he saw no future for a civilization that could perpetrate the atrocities it did against the human spirit, and yet retain the velleities displayed by governments and mass communication agencies. He had the perception that too many people were involved in the decline, that it was not merely a 'conspiracy' by some political interest. Thus he could end an essay on Charles Dickens with the following pregnant phrases:

It is the face of a man who is always fighting against something, but who fights in the open and is not frightened, the face of a man who is *generously angry* – in other words, of a nineteenth century liberal, a free intelligence, a type hated with equal hatred by all the smelly little orthodoxies which are now contending for our souls.

Animal Farm is Orwell's great work, treating the betrayal of a utopian vision by those who claimed to be its defenders. In *Nineteen Eighty-Four* Orwell figured the corrupted ideal at a later stage, when power had become centralized, and human beings struggled to keep alive values of decency and truth in a world of lies and deceit. The earlier work has a piquancy the latter does not have, since it works at the primary level of moral fable, re-enacting the myth of the fall in the context of an animal story through which the reader sees the outline of events in Russia from 1917 to the consolidation of Stalinism in the 1930s.

Another advantage of the animal fable is the opportunity it gave Orwell for individual characterization. The various kinds of animals serve admirably to suggest the different types of humanity present in a cross-section of society. The reader might not be aware at first that the prize boar, Old Major, stands for one of the Fathers of the Socialist movement – he is, perhaps, not simply Karl Marx, but a kind of amalgam of the great figures of nineteenth-century revolutionary radicalism, here vividly personalized. The message Old Major assembles the farm animals to hear in the first chapter artfully implies the populist elements in the socialist creed, in the folklore myth of a countryside in which all are equal and none are exploiters. Old Major's speech is in fact affecting exactly because of its apparent origin in the folk-memory: it is presented as a dream, in which Old Major remembers the full words of the song 'Beasts of

England', 'words, I am certain, which were sung by animals of long ago and have been lost to memory for generations'. The song is a millennial vision of the overthrow of 'Tyrant Man' and the creation of the perfect society in which all are free – 'And the fruitful fields of England / Shall be trod by beasts alone'.

The song is taken up by the animals – the pigs and dogs, Animal Farm's future masters, learn it the readiest. It resounds through the events that follow, for it represents of course the pure, utopian vision, the inspirational socialist faith that hangs like a rainbow over the squalid tale of butchery and deceit soon perpetrated in its name. Conservative champions of *Animal Farm* often forget Orwell's socialism, and thus miss the poignancy of the work, for the author too had been caught by the vision of a socialist utopia, and the last thing he aimed at was to dim that vision.

After the death of Old Major his doctrines are comprehended in 'Animalism', and expounded by the cleverest animals, the pigs. There are two leaders, Napoleon – who stands for Stalin – and Snowball – who represents Trotsky. Napoleon has 'a reputation for getting his way', while Snowball is 'more vivacious . . . quicker in speech and more inventive', though less deep. Napoleon, as it transpires, is the better organizer, while Snowball's inventiveness eventually proves his down-fall.

Mr Jones is eventually caught napping underneath a copy of *News of the World*, and is driven off the farm after a short battle. The animals sing 'Beasts of England', but still cannot believe the farm is now really their own. The pigs at once codify the principles of Animalism, which are painted on the big barn by Snowball. These are The Seven Commandments, and they act as a major point of reference in the story, as one by one the ideals of the revolution are perverted and broken by the pigs. Almost immediately, the pigs claim their first privilege while the other animals are working: an enormous amount of milk is given by the cows, only to be surreptitiously consumed by the pigs.

In the early days of the revolution the animals are united by a spirit of comradeship, for the first time reaping the harvest for themselves. Education in the principles of Animalism, and political meetings in the great barn to discuss the workings of the farm, are regularly conducted despite the fact that the majority of animals are too stupid to understand them. Enmity between Napoleon and Snowball becomes a feature of all schemes for the farm. The pigs produce an apologist for their leadership in Squealer, who is a kind of Minister for Propaganda and comes to justify every perversion of Animalism successfully because the animals can never understand his sophistry. Thus on the assumption by the pigs of special rations for themselves:

'Comrades!' he cried. 'You do not imagine, I hope, that we pigs are doing this in a spirit of selfishness and privilege? Many of us actually dislike milk and apples. I dislike them myself. Our sole object in taking these things is to preserve our health. Milk and apples (this has been proved by Science, comrades) contain substances absolutely necessary to the well-being of a pig. We pigs are brain-workers. The whole management and organization of this farm depends on us. Day and night we are watching over your welfare. It is for *your* sake that we drink that milk and eat those apples. Do you know what would happen if we pigs failed in our duty? Jones would come back! Yes, Jones would come back! Surely, comrades,' cried Squealer almost pleadingly, skipping from side to side and whisking his tail, 'surely there is no one among you who wants to see Jones come back?'

Such an exposure of the genre of lying propaganda Orwell had himself experienced when fighting alongside the Communists in Spain gains its effectiveness from the egregious character of the pig. It is perfectly fitted to the fabliau genre, readily appreciated in the many literary traditions, from France to Persia, in which the fable is well known.

Similar to the fashion in which the European capitalist powers supported the White Russians in the Civil War of 1919–21, the neighbouring farmers equip Jones with a force to regain his farm and extirpate the intolerable creed of Animalism. The animals repel this force, Snowball and Boxer, the sturdy cart-horse who stands for the faithful, if simple, party supporter, in particular manifesting great heroism and receiving medals in recognition. Thus two events are subscribed on the calendar – the anniversaries of the Rebellion and successful defence of the Rebellion respectively. But there soon follows an event of fateful significance for the revolution. Snowball draws up plans for the construction of a windmill that would bring electricity and a new standard of living to the farm. Napoleon, fearing to be outmanoeuvred by his rival, opposes the plan, and just when it appears the vote will go against him, he brings in some ferocious dogs that he has had privately raised. Snowball is driven out, and democracy is ended. Napoleon now takes the full reins of power, cowering any opposition through his murderous dogs (Stalin's hated secret police, the *Cheka*) – thus the great schism between Trotsky and Stalin. Henceforth the role of Snowball in the revolution is successively distorted until he is portrayed as an agent of Jones from the start, and number one traitor to Animal Farm. The animals, at first bewildered and unsure, receive their first lesson in political re-education from Squealer. Napoleon, he tells them, had been in favour of the windmill all along – in fact had created the plans himself, only opposing them as a means of getting rid of Snowball. ' "Tactics, comrades, tactics!" skipping round and whisking his tail with a merry laugh. The animals were not certain what the word meant, but Squealer spoke so persuasively, and the three dogs who happened to be with him growled so threateningly, that they accepted his explanation without further questions.'

One by one, Orwell figures the events that corrupted the socialist revolution in Russia. The conditions of work grow harder but the animals bear them for the sake of the revolution. Then they learn that Napoleon has got an agent – a human being – in order to do trade with the outside world. All is sacrificed to the construction of the windmill (standing for Stalin's forced industrialization of the Soviet Union in the 1930s). But at the same time, the pigs begin to sleep in beds, even though this is forbidden by the Seven Commandments. Squealer informs the other animals that what had been meant was that no animal should sleep between sheets, for otherwise anywhere an animal went to sleep could be called its 'bed'. The windmill is successfully completed only to be destroyed in a storm. Napoleon tells the animals that this is Snowball's work, that Snowball had left his footprints in the direction of Foxwood Farm. Yet the animals begin the work over again under terrible hardship, only to be faced with the first slaughter of their number – some of the hens who refused to give up their eggs to be sold to Whymper, the agent. (The hens probably represent the richer peasant class, the *kulaks* whom Stalin virtually eliminated because of their opposition to his collectivization of agriculture.)

The animals are astounded to hear that Snowball was a traitor from the beginning, that even his heroism at the Battle of the Cowshed against Jones was an illusion. To force home the point, the animals are called upon to confess complicity with Snowball against Animal Farm, and there follow terrible executions of those who do confess. These actions, involving the killing of animal by animal, greatly depress the remaining animals, already confused by the confessions of traitorship. Some go to the hill overlooking the farm and ruminate sadly on the turn of events. The mare Clover is dismayed:

If she could have spoken her thoughts, it would have been to say that this was not what they had aimed at when they had set themselves years ago to work for the overthrow of the human race. These scenes of terror and slaughter were not what they had looked forward to on that night when Old Major first stirred them to rebellion. If she herself had had any picture of the future, it had been of a society of animals set free from hunger and the whip, all equal, each working according to his capacity, the strong protecting the weak, as she had protected the last brood of ducklings with her foreleg on the night of Major's speech. Instead – she did not know why – they had come to a time when no one dared speak his mind, when fierce, growling dogs roamed everywhere, and when you had to watch your comrades torn to pieces after confessing to shocking crimes.

From this moment onwards the pigs do as they like, breaking the Commandments at will, with Squealer to justify each example of duplicity. Morale within the farm is maintained by hate campaigns against the other farms, with the exception of the one Napoleon has as his ally. The cult of leadership is enacted around Napoleon, who is nevertheless humorously compromised when farmer Frederick reneges on a deal by sending forged banknotes. A war ensues in which the windmill is again destroyed, but the invaders are repulsed. Though a great cost to Animal Farm, Napoleon declares this a victory, and the pigs get drunk on Mr Jones's whisky. Daily, the pigs appear more like human beings, and so, though not before the terrible betrayal of Boxer who is callously sent to the knackers in a disguised van when he has outlived his usefulness, the way is cleared for the last irony, now long expected. A pig is seen walking on its hindlegs – thus departing from the last shibboleth of Animalism: 'four legs good, two legs bad'. Then the change of the Commandments, to Orwell's *coup de grâce*: 'All animals are equal but some are more equal than others.' The installation of the new governing class is made explicit by the arrival of Pilkington and other farmers to inspect Manor Farm – for the name has been changed back to its original. Toasts are exchanged, but as the disbelieving animals look on unnoticed from outside, an altercation breaks out over a card game: 'The creatures outside looked from pig to man, and from man to pig, and from pig to man again; but already it was impossible to say which was which.'

This short, satirical fable has been read in the western world as a damning indictment of Communism, but in fact it is no less scathing about the capitalist countries – the farms run by the human beings, whom the pigs merely succeed in aping, and who are portrayed as consistently selfish and devious. The message of *Animal Farm* is that in this world the honest and less intelligent, as well as the ignorant, will be continually duped by the leaders. In this Orwell's vision lives up to the pessimism of his other work, being a condemnation of politics as a whole, but all the same an avowal of his faith in the meek and humble of the earth. Orwell's position, despite his agnosticism, is deeply founded in Christian idealism, a potent influence upon British socialism from Owen through Ruskin, to Philip Snowden and James Maxton. In the even more pessimistic *Nineteen Eighty-Four* Orwell puts his hope in the 'proles', in the form of a grotesquely fat washer-woman – hardly an idealized proletarian figure, and surely beyond politicization. Oddly, in outward terms, Orwell's last writings suggest he was groping for some kind of mystic intuition to carry him through the nightmare impasse of twentieth-century political and social history. The prole woman was a symbol of vitalism, and the hero and heroine in *Nineteen Eighty-Four* find their exultation in human love before this is destroyed in the nightmare of room 101. Orwell was too scrupulous to seek escape from the nightmare-vision through some manufactured mysticism, as did Huxley. But the impression left by his work is of an embryonic spiritual ideal that emerges from his profound bedrock of moral honesty and commitment to truth. Orwell insists on the necessity of a social ethic – this constituted his religion, as far as he had any; but his humility and honesty cannot be lost on those who see the answer to the nightmare in a social philosophy founded upon a spiritual love.

A writer who had experienced Communism at even closer quarters than Orwell is Arthur Koestler, a Hungarian and former Communist. Koestler wrote *Darkness at Noon* on the eve of the Second World War. Where Orwell forsook a probing philosophical analysis of the reasons for the corruption of the revolutionary socialist ideal of Utopia, using instead a trenchant satire to give a sharp-edged picture of the moral evils perpetrated in its name, Koestler chose exactly that philosophical approach. In *Darkness at Noon* there is no stage by stage account of the process of corruption; rather, the revolution is encountered two decades after its first triumph, and now in a process of consolidation. It is the mid-nineteen-thirties, and the scene is the Soviet Union as seen through the mind of a veteran Bolshevik and revolutionary leader, now in disgrace, on the verge of committal for political 'crimes'. In fact the dilemma facing Rubashov is whether to assist the authorities, admit his guilt, and so aid the consolidation of the party's version of the revolution, or to stand out vainly but nobly for his own view. As Rubashov turns this over in his mind in his prison cell, he remembers his past activities on behalf of the revolutionary cause, and this involves him in questioning the whole validity of his own motivation, and by implication, that of the revolution itself.

The subtlety of Koestler's novel rests in his portrayal of his central character. Rubashov is not a romantic revolutionary idealist, a man betrayed by the corruption of a nobly strived-for ideal. He is almost as guilty as his gaolers for the road the revolution has taken, for he too has dealt in expediency and ruthless sophistry, sacrificing others, including a one-time mistress, in the name of revolutionary exigency. His self-questioning does not however take the form of bitter remorse and searching guilt – he is a wholly committed revolutionary, in the mould of Lenin who ate, drank and dreamt revolution. He is convinced of the necessity of a scientific basis for the tactics of revolution – and a 'scientific' approach means the utter abandonment of personal scruples and ethical considerations of any kind. The individual's own sense of personal identity is a 'grammatical fiction' – that is to say, the use of 'I' has no meaning. All is sacrificed in the name of the triumph of the proletariat, which is to be pursued in the certainty of its inevitability. The revolutionary is convinced of his discovery of the 'laws of history', and this certitude absolves him of any responsibility other than to the correct prosecution of the revolution. It is in fact his failure in this respect which first causes Rubashov to question his past.

It is true that he had not been completely devoid of scruples – he had suffered vague feelings of disquiet before, but these of their very nature (as mere feelings) were hardly worthy of analysis – until he found himself in prison, and on the verge of liquidation. He had been imprisoned before, in Germany, but that had been at the hands of the enemy, and he had been freed in a diplomatic deal to return home as a hero. Yet his previous experience of prison is the focus through which, in the first pages of the book, Rubashov is able to come to terms with his new predicament. Expecting to be tortured and beaten, Rubashov finds himself ignored – with time on his hands, he starts to consider his past career.

A veteran of the revolution of 1917, Rubashov had risen to the heights of the party and had gained the esteem of the rank and file. He had been sent abroad, first to deliver the party line to members of the movement in other countries, then as diplomat in Germany. Now Rubashov remembers incidents which had somewhat disquieted him at the time, but which now take on the complexion of betrayals. First there had been the young party member in Germany whom he had been sent to instruct in the aftermath of the decimation of the Communists by the Nazis in 1933 (in fact Koestler only implies – he does not explicitly state – these facts). The young man had insisted that Rubashov's orders were impossible, given the harassed nature of the party members in Germany – Rubashov had reluctantly argued a little, then, aware of the young man's unreliability in the party's terms, had expelled him and caused him to be arrested. Then there had been the veteran comrade in Belgium who was leader of Communist dockers in a particular port. Rubashov had been instructed to win the dockers over to the new line – previously they had been instructed to boycott supplies to the enemy, preventing them from getting through. Now they had to be won over to handling supplies destined to the very same enemy (clearly one of the Fascist powers) – sent by the homeland of the revolution. Such a trade was pragmatic, necessary to the survival of the Soviet Union – the dockers were at first incredulous of what was being asked of them, only the old man understood. Finally he walked out of the meeting – and was later found hanged. These kinds of volte-faces accurately reflect the shifting foreign policies of the Soviet Union that culminated in the 1939 Russo-German pact that shocked so many supporters and erstwhile admirers of Communist Russia.

Rubashov's disquiet over these occurrences begins to turn less on the tactics behind them than on the unease arising from the cold sacrifice of honest, simple devotees of the revolution. This is highlighted in Rubashov's remembering of his treatment of his secretary – a plump, quiet girl whom he took as his mistress, but did nothing to defend after she had been denounced as politically untrustworthy. Because Rubashov's own career would have been seriously implicated had he stood up for her, he had remained silent. The sacrifice of Arlova leaves the imprisoned revolutionary with a 'tormenting sense of guilt'.

Eventually Rubashov is brought for interrogation. He finds his interrogator is an old comrade, Ivanov, a man schooled in the same political experiences as himself. Though at first he suspects Ivanov, Rubashov comes round to his arguments, and is ready to sign a confession of guilt when Ivanov is replaced by a younger man, Gletkin. This Gletkin is a child of the revolution; having come to maturity afterwards, he is of a different generation from Rubashov and Ivanov. The older men, hardened revolutionaries, had retained a form of cynical detachment even from the course of the revolution itself – they were able to argue over the matter of tactics – the dispensing with men and policies – in a tone of logic tempered with light melancholy. Ivanov had informed Gletkin that his crude methods of interrogation would not suit Rubashov, who would only succumb to ideological logic; Ivanov argues with Rubashov that he is *de facto* defeated, that his logical path is to sacrifice himself by admitting his guilt, so aiding the revolution. Convinced of his defeat and the worthlessness of heroic gestures, Rubashov determines to sign a confession, only to find his new interrogator embarking on a technique of psychological violence. Gletkin favours wearing down his victim by means of powerful lights and sleep withdrawal – Rubashov is worn down and signs abject confessions not out of logical conviction, but mental and physical exhaustion.

Rubashov's dialogues with himself, and with his two interrogators, constitute the philosophic search into the corruption of the revolution which is the basis of Koestler's novel. Rubashov struggles to ascertain where he and his fellow revolutionaries went wrong; Ivanov and Gletkin, from different standpoints, maintain that the revolution is on course. To Rubashov it seems that the conundrum behind the failure of the revolution lies somewhere about the complicated process of turning aims into fact:

All our principles were right, but our results were wrong. This is a diseased century. We diagnosed the disease and its causes with microscopic exactness, but whenever we applied the healing knife a new sore appeared. Our will was hard and pure, we should have been loved by the people. But they hate us. Why are we so odious and detested?

We brought you truth, and in our mouths it sounded a lie. We brought you freedom, and it looks in our hands like a whip. We brought you the living life, and where our voice is heard the trees wither and there is a rustling of dry leaves . . .

In his conversation with Ivanov, Rubashov phrases the question again:

. . . we had descended into the depths, into the formless, anonymous masses, which at all times constituted the substance of history; and we were the first to discover the laws of her motion. We had discovered the laws of her inertia, of the slow changing of her molecular structure, and of her sudden eruptions . . . We dug in the primeval mud of history and there we found her laws. We knew more than ever men have known about mankind; that is why our revolution succeeded. And now you have buried it all again.

According to Rubashov, the party no longer represents the masses; it seems that in order to achieve the ideals for which the revolution was made, the new regime has introduced measures more arduous than during the old regime. Work conditions are worse and repression is greater. Rubashov remembers how the old revolutionaries began to disappear one by one, how their portraits disappeared from old photographs and their text-books were withdrawn. The reality of all this is brought home to Rubashov when he witnesses an old comrade being taken through the prison corridors to his execution.

Rubashov eventually begins to realize that the cause of the nightmare is to be located in the means used by the revolutionaries; Ivanov contests: 'The principle that the end justifies the means is and remains the only rule of political ethics.' Ivanov justifies the liquidation of the *kulaks* on the grounds that it was a 'surgical operation'. Similarly, party officials who followed wrong or unsuccessful policies had likewise to be disposed of. This he terms experimental – those who squeamishly question it display 'anti-vivisection morality'. Rubashov himself finds it difficult to overcome these so-called 'scientific' ways of thinking. In his diary he tries to explain the terrible events of Stalinist Russia in terms of 'the relative maturity of the masses' – a theory that sees processes of important change as inevitably painful. Only in his last hours before execution does he leave such notions behind, and begin to see himself as a spiritual being on the verge of a great unknown – death.

It is Rubashov's experience of Gletkin's crude methods of interrogation that eventually breaks his adherence to revolutionary thought. Gletkin represents a new generation of Communist, freed from even the humanity of an Ivanov. 'Truth is what is useful to humanity, falsehood what is harmful', he says. So he justifies telling the masses palpable lies in order to have greater influence over them. He says that Rubashov must confess to the most abject crimes he did not commit, because he represents a defeated faction of the party which must be shown to be utterly discredited. Rubashov knows that Gletkin is merely following on his own methods, but now he sees the stark horror behind the language of scientific theory. Before his execution he solves the conundrum he has thrown over in his mind since his arrest:

It was a mistake in the system; perhaps it lay in the precept which until now he had held to be uncontestable, in whose name he had sacrificed others and was himself being sacrificed: in the precept, that the end justifies the means. It was this sentence which had killed the great fraternity of the Revolution and made them all run amuck. What had he once written in his diary? 'We have thrown overboard all conventions, our sole guiding principle is that of consequent logica; we are sailing without ethical ballast.'

Perhaps the heart of the evil lay there. Perhaps it did not suit mankind to sail without ballast. And perhaps reason alone was a defective compass, which led one on such a winding, twisted course that the goal finally disappeared in the mist.

Perhaps now would come the time of great darkness.

Still Rubashov holds to a vestige of evolutionary thought:

perhaps in the distant future party men will turn into monks and court purity. Perhaps one day society would turn to the 'oceanic sense', that sense of transcendent awe that past mystics had spoken of. Thus *Darkness At Noon* turns from nightmare to a distant mystic goal.

The work of Orwell and Koestler, then, laid the foundations of our perception of the horrendous failure of the revolutionary socialist experiment. They provided the basic principles, and a later writer, Alexander Solzhenitsyn, has filled in much more detail from his own experience as an inmate of a Stalinist prison camp. Inevitably, because writing about a political system always involves a polarization of some sort amongst readers – or, more precisely, those who are prejudiced not to read as against those who are prejudiced *to* read – there will still be many who will not accept the truth in these writers. Orwell himself was under no illusions about the capacity for objectivity among fellow-travellers. Few highly educated people in the West are as gullible about Communist Russia today as Shaw was nearly fifty years ago. Still the vogue for revolutionary socialism persists among the young. They, truly, perceive what they wish to perceive, and again Orwell would have not been at all surprised at their doing so. Twentieth-century history teaches no lesson more clearly than that every new generation learns almost nothing from the experiences of the previous one.

But we must not be partial in our perception either. To look at the alternative utopias afforded by the West is to see no conspicuous success. Indeed, it has long been apparent that the superiority of the so-called 'Free World' rests mainly in its economic achievements. People are lured from the Eastern bloc to the capitalist West for the sake of freedom no doubt, but above all what they seek, and we cannot blame them for this, is Eldorado. It is for this reason that so many immigrants have arrived in the United States.

There has been no more pungent a critic of the United States and its social *mores* than Henry Miller, arguably the greatest American writer of the modern age. Miller is in his own way a fine American and a patriot; he has written with unparalleled vigour of his youth in Brooklyn, before and immediately after the Great War. But he is also atypical of so much we have come to understand by American culture. Miller may still have as his main claim to fame some of the notoriety he earned as author of *Tropic of Cancer* and *Tropic of Capricorn*. His use of strongly-flavoured language is not the most important feature of his work though. Miller's view of the world in fact puts him in the company of European Romanticism, for he is a lover of nature and art, and his writing displays a vitalistic insistence upon visionary intensity. Miller has the rare genius of seeing the world through his own eyes and not through the eyes of others; he loves the bizarre, and glories in the heroic rebellion against poverty and insensitivity when he sees it, especially in the humblest. This outlook has made him a friend of the Black and of the American Indian, and it lends his work a moving dignity that might surprise those who are otherwise dissuaded by his reputation. Above all, Miller detests the inhumanity of capitalism, its hatred of individuality and spontaneity, its sick debasement of the image of God within us all.

Miller's explosive, apocalyptic style of writing is reminiscent of Thomas Carlyle's vitriolic denunciation of the Victorian free-market economy and his contemporaries' blind worship of vulgar success, in *The Latter-Day Pamphlets*. There is a marvellous section in *Tropic of Capricorn* describing Miller's experience of working as manager for an American messenger service in one of the great cities. He is appalled by the wastage of human material caused by his bosses' instructions to hire and fire at a consistently large turn-over. All the flotsam and jetsam of American society pass through their employ – and almost all the nationalities of the world. Miller is scornful of the American claim to be the melting-pot of humanity. He sees American society as a Moloch, devouring human beings in pursuit of all that is useless, vulgar and ugly. In his observations on America, *The Air-Conditioned Nightmare*, a book written after travels throughout the United States in the early nineteen-forties, Miller concludes that modern America has in fact destroyed the traces of every culture of beauty that preceded it on the continent of North America. The first white settlers murdered and corrupted the Indians, who lived in harmony with the earth and possessed a profound folklore. Progressively, the old influences (including the Spanish, and the French as seen in New Orleans) disappeared:

Less than a hundred years has elapsed since this jewel of America faded out. It seems more like a thousand. Everything that was of beauty, significance or promise has been destroyed and buried in the avalanche of false progress. In the thousand years of almost incessant war Europe has not lost what we have lost in a hundred years of 'peace and progress'. No foreign enemy ruined the South. No barbaric vandals devastated the great tracts of land which are as barren and hideous as the dead surface of the moon. We can't attribute to the Indians the transformation of a peaceful, slumbering island like Manhattan into the most hideous city in the world . . .

Less than two hundred years ago a great social experiment was begun on this virgin continent. The Indians whom we dispossessed, decimated and reduced to the status of outcasts . . . had a reverent attitude towards the land . . . They lived in communion with Nature on what we choose to call a low level of life. Though they possessed no written language they were poetic to the core and deeply religious. Our forefathers came along and, seeking refuge from their oppressors, began by poisoning the Indians with alcohol and venereal disease, by raping their women and murdering their children. The wisdom of life which the Indians possessed they scorned and denigrated. When they had finally completed their work of conquest and extermination they herded the miserable remnants of a great race into concentration camps and proceeded to break what spirit was left in them.

Miller goes on to portray the United States as an empire of crass materialism: 'Radio, telephone, cinema, newspaper, pulp magazine, fountain-pen, wrist-watch, vacuum cleaner, or other gadgets ad infinitum. Are these the baubles that make life worthwhile? Are these what makes us happy, carefree, generous-hearted, sympathetic, kindly, peaceful and Godly?' America has been satirized for its materialism at greater length since, and in the forty years since Miller was writing it has advanced many miles further into the quagmire of consumerism, poisoning in the process the European countries that

Miller greatly admired. The 'nightmare' that Miller experienced has since acquired television as its ultimate soporific of the soul. But it has also remained true that American culture has hardly arisen above mediocrity, has given mankind no great tradition of Art, Music or Philosophy, but continues to persuade its young to do 'something practical'. Even the 'hippy' rebellion of the late sixties revealed again the basic materialism ingrained in the soul of America, in its pursuit of nirvana through drugs and free love.

Miller prophesied that America would have to undergo a catastrophe, a national humiliation. He wrote in the 1940s:

It may be true that this is the great melting-pot of the world. But the fusion has not begun to take place yet. Only when the red man and the black man, the brown man and the yellow man unite with the white peoples of the earth in full equality, in full amity and respect for one another, will the melting pot serve its purpose. Then we may see on this continent – thousands of years hence – the beginnings of a new order of life. But the white American will first have to be humiliated and defeated; he will have to humble himself and cry for mercy; he will have to acknowledge his omissions; he will have to beg and pray that he be admitted to the new and greater fraternity of mankind which he himself was incapable of creating.

And again:

When the destruction brought about by the Second World War is complete another sort of destruction will set in. And it will be far more drastic, far more terrible than the destruction which we are now witnessing. The whole planet will be in the throes of revolution. And the fires will rage until the very foundations of this present world crumble. Then we shall see whether the ability to make money and the ability to survive are one and the same. Then we shall see the meaning of true wealth.

(Henry Miller's prognostications for America, which are very similar to those of the Bahá'í Faith, might lead us to wonder if there was any contact. Miller writes of visiting the Bahá'í Temple in Wilmette, where he was impressed by the peace it inspired. He liked the absence of racial discrimination in Bahá'í teaching, and wrote: 'It is for this reason that the Bahá'í movement is destined to outlast all the other religious organizations on this continent.')

When we review the range of work that exists on the failure of twentieth-century experiments to create terrestrial paradise, inevitably we come again to one work written earlier than most of the others, in 1932; it is Aldous Huxley's satire of Utopia to end all utopias, *Brave New World*. Huxley's work has retained its significance even after fifty years because it continues to speak of a society which in essence is so in keeping with the dreams of the technocrats and men of power who have done most to lay the course of this century. Moreover, Huxley's satire day by day acquires more disquietingly a truth to the life we are living. And indeed there is every reason, given Huxley's genius and imagination, to have expected this; the second half of the twentieth century has gone on building ever more surely upon the foundations laid by the Prophets of Brave New World: particularly the production of endless uniformity on a massive scale inaugurated by Henry Ford. For Huxley's prescience lay in his realization that it was not to be political philosophers or revolutionary fanatics who would determine the new world, but planners, aided and abetted by the men who could control the human mind, and crush the spirit of man under the regimen of uniformity and conformity. *Brave New World* is politically totalitarian like the Fascist and Communist states, but its basic philosophy is closer to the capitalist aspirations of the United States: the creation of a society in which everyone indulges his appetite to the fullest, stimulated by the promise of agelessness, surrounded by triviality and an intellectual environment suitable for ten-year-olds. There is no need to wield the instruments of terror in order to ensure conformity; conditioning from birth has made it possible, in the words of the Director of Hatcheries and Conditioning, '[to make] people like their unescapable social destiny'.

This world state, we are told, arose out of the ruins of the old order, after general war and economic collapse. Dissidents were at first oppressed, but the development of suggestion techniques – hypnosis practised while asleep, from childhood –

made such crude methods unnecessary. The aim of the controllers of the new society was stability – 'The primal and the ultimate need'. They were further aided by breakthroughs in the field of Eugenics, enabling a kind of mass production of human beings in test tubes – for the family has been completely suppressed and replaced. A caste system was created which was again based upon Eugenics: rough and sturdy types for what menial tasks remained, intellectually stultified, and conditioned to accept their lot; an ascending scale upwards to the top caste – Alpha plus – which is physically attractive and intellectually developed. Individuality is offset by the production of multiple, identical types in any one batch. After this treatment, the single human is further integrated into uniformity by all kinds of group activities, from the surrogate for religion, the 'Community Song', to outdoor sports, like 'Obstacle Golf'. Above all, the individual is released from sexual inhibition: promiscuity becomes the convention, the encouraged norm; new batches of humans are taught the slogan: 'Everyone belongs to everyone else.' Young children are taught to engage in erotic play in preparation for a sex life that will continue unweakened until their death – for the old retain all the vigour and beauty of youth, only succumbing suddenly to their ends, which they have been conditioned not to fear, again from childhood. When depression threatens, the individual takes a 'soma holiday' – a few capsules of the drug called soma leaving no after-effects, and carrying the mind into a world of tension-free fulfilment of desire. The secret behind the stability of this society is its answering to every need of the human being; all struggle and striving, frustration and pain are eliminated. The construction and content of human life have been profoundly changed: the world of endless suffering, of craving for unsatisfied desire, of death and re-birth into the perennial cycle, the world perceived by Gautama Buddha and experienced by the entire human race from its creation until now – all that has been abolished! And the remarkable fact about Huxley's utopia is that he makes us believe it is possible.

Since *Brave New World* was written Western society has year by year been reducing the number of techniques behind the stability of that utopia which Western society is unable to implement potentially. Huxley pre-figured the post-war world of television advertising, the methods used by the 'hidden persuaders' to create demand for their products. Technology has advanced to the state where the world of luxury suggested in the novel is within the experience of some at least of the inhabitants of Western society. The cinema has responded almost to the letter to Huxley's cinema of sex and thrills – the 'feelies'. The drugs industry has undergone an efflorescence. Even the theories have been in the process of realization: divorce and free love, the disintegration of the family, large-scale contraceptive availability, TV-style evangelism in America – the list could be greatly enlarged.

Indeed, what prevents Huxley's utopia from becoming reality? Eugenics of the kind he imagined is not beyond the future scope of science. The mind-benders have already flexed their brain muscles. Culture and orthodox religion are fast becoming a memory to the new generations. The demand for ever more varied pleasure grows daily. In fact, what seems to stand in the way is the very barbarism Huxley consigned to the past: warfare, oppression, sheer social wastefulness. Perhaps we are merely awaiting the collapse already mentioned for a *Brave New World* type of world society to emerge from the ruins of the present age.

Huxley's novel assumes a kind of twilight reader – a person still in command of the cultural achievements of European civilization, yet cynically aware of the onset of mass society. In his early satirical novels Huxley had appeared content to laugh at this emerging world in the company of brilliant, Bloomsbury-like intellectuals and beauties. There was too an underlying weariness, a sense of purposelessness comparable to the poetry of Eliot, but less obvious. *Brave New World* continues the satirical vision of what Huxley later described as 'the amused, Pyrrhonic aesthete' – amused, because the author remains detached, 'Pyrrhonic', because he is also aware that he would have no place in such a society. The intelligence and wit of the thinker bristles through the work: characters have unlikely amalgam-names drawn from the illuminae of the 1920s and early thirties – 'Lenina', 'Benito Hoover', 'Polly Trotsky'. Henry Ford has replaced the deity, and the appearance of the model-T is the equivalent of the hegira in the dating of history. Pavlov has given his name to the hatcheries and conditioning centres; Freud is behind the taboos of the new society – parenthood and monogamy. The Director of Hatcheries speaks with assumed ease about the experiments of so-and-so, in the tones of confident, ebullient early twentieth-century science. It is indeed a world of scientific and social positivism, calling upon us to remember guiltily the gusto with which we once read H. G. Wells.

In the state of endless repetition the new society affords there rests the successful completion of Henry Ford's promise to free mankind from the shackles of its sordid past. 'History is bunk' – Huxley skilfully highlights the saying, for does there not lie behind it all the arrogance of the planners of our own time, all the contempt for the cycle of nature and the harmony of the universe that man-centred maniacs in the twentieth century have taken as their inspiration to plunder the earth, and poison the roots of our existence? It is a hideous saying, and its horror echoes through the novel, informing the basic story of three men's search for release from the nightmare of mindless hedonism.

Bernard Marx, the stunted Alpha-plus who has unsocial grudges and the wish, at first, to escape from Utopia, is the catalyst behind events. He takes his girl-friend – for whom he has unsocial desires of possession – to the savage reservation in New Mexico. He sees there the alternative alone open to misfits from civilization: a backward, superstitious tribal society, living in dirt and amidst disease, old age, and frightening death. His female companion undergoes the whole experience as a terrible nightmare. But Marx discovers a young savage and his mother – the woman having come out from civilization with a high-ranking official, Bernard's boss, got lost, and been left to bear his child in squalor. Marx, realizing the leverage his discovery will afford him back in civilization, takes the pair back. There he has the satisfaction of destroying his boss because of the opprobrium of parentage, and is fêted by the powerful for the sake of meeting the savage. But the savage is horrified by the brave new world, and when he falls in love with Marx's ex-girlfriend, he displays the symptoms of passionate unrequited love, which turn to wild asceticism when she offers her favours in the promiscuous style of her society. The savage, who has educated himself by reading a copy of Shakespeare he found on the reservation, is the reference point for everything denied by the utopia. He thinks and speaks in heightened, poetic imagery, quoting liberally and unaffectedly from Shakespeare. He is religious and conscience-stricken. He loves his hag of a mother. His revulsion from his new world leads to Marx's loss of favour, and incidents that upset the peace of society, and finally end in an interview with the Controller.

Marx, together with his friend and fellow dissident, the brilliant Helmholtz, are exiled by the Controller for their part in the savage's desperado forays against the social order. During the interview the savage argues for his state of freedom against the Controller's defence of his society's achievements. The debate centres on the savage's disparagement of the 'feelies' in favour of the drama of *Othello*. The Controller replies:

. . . our world is not the same as Othello's world. You can't make flivvers without steel – and you can't make tragedies without social instability. The world's stable now. People are happy; they get what they want, and they never want what they can't get. They're well off; they're safe; they're never ill; they're not afraid of death; they're blissfully ignorant of passion and old age; they're plagued with no mothers or fathers; they've got no wives, or children, or lovers to feel strongly about; they're so conditioned that they practically can't help behaving as they ought to behave. And if anything should go wrong, there's *soma*.

The Controller admits that happiness is not as stirring as 'the glamour of a good fight against misfortune, [has] none of the picturesqueness of a struggle with temptation, or a fatal overthrow by passion or doubt. Happiness is never grand.' But this is the price of stability, and really, if we were to be honest, to our Sancho Panza selves this does not seem so great a price. It is the world presented to us by the colour supplements and the TV advertisements, except they have yet to dispense with the outmoded notions of family, wife, husband and children. And as the Controller says, in reality these are exactly the causes of our main discomfiture – replace these, ensure employment and settled surroundings, and most of man's striving would be ended. We are at a far remove from Herbert's poem in which man is given everything by God except rest to enjoy this. And indeed the Controller has an answer to the old religious frame of mind – he quotes from Newman: 'The religious sentiment will compensate us for our losses' – and adds:

But there aren't any losses for us to compensate; religious sentiment is superfluous. And why should we go hunting for a substitute for youthful desires, when youthful desires never fail? A substitute for distractions, when we go on enjoying all the old fooleries to the very last? What need have we of repose when our minds and bodies continue to delight in activity? of consolation, when we have *soma*? of something immovable, when there is the social order?

Here is a perfect summary of the aims of hedonism – for if life were so controlled that all the pleasures of the senses could be acquired with none of the hangovers, then surely paradise would be at hand? This is the victory that utilitarianism foresees, and Huxley is right in figuring this paradise as aesthetically awful, instead of a feast to our higher faculties as is Morris's utopian vision, in *News From Nowhere*. For great art, as the Controller says, has to be sacrificed for the feelies and the scent organ, the implication being that a paradise of the senses is also a mindless one. It is flatly impossible to have Beethoven's *Missa Solemnis* (a thanksgiving to the Creator born out of the composer's experience of deafness) in a paradise where pain is unknown. It is thus a stroke of genius that leads Huxley to put into the mouth of the Controller the following answer to the savage's enquiry, 'how does God manifest himself?':

. . . he manifests himself as an absence; as though he weren't there at all.

And this, according to Huxley, is the inevitable concomitant of an age of materialistic achievement: 'God isn't compatible with machinery and scientific medicine and happiness.' Every argument the savage uses against the Controller's world of ease and order comes up against the same riposte: this is unhealthy and so we have abolished it. The savage wishes to have the Pascalian world of flawed perfection, of canker and rose. The Controller is disgusted by the inefficiency and waste they involve. Society has been so ordered as to banish God along with imperfection. The savage cries out in the words used by every Romantic artist since the creation of the first machine of the industrial revolution:

But I don't want comfort. I want God, I want poetry, I want real danger, I want freedom, I want goodness. I want sin.

Brave New World is a novel of singular importance to our time then. Whether the society it envisages will ever come about we do not know; its importance rests in its summary of the aims of materialistic hedonism. The suicide of the savage at the end of the novel – not to speak of the relentlessness with which he is pursued by the media and titillated sightseers – expresses Huxley's pessimism as well as his own assessment of the actual import of the nightmare world he has envisaged. But the philosophical conundrum at the heart of the work is as profound as Koestler's discussion of the problem of ends and means: it is, can we balance our desire for material progress, for control over our habitat and thus ourselves, with the spiritual needs which the founders of our age have denied?

There have been countless diagnoses of the sicknesses at the heart of the modern world, and it would be vain to repeat them here, or to add another. It suffices to observe the common strands that emerge from the authors we have discussed. In Orwell's utopia, an experiment in socialist equality subverted by the more intelligent caste who soon tyrannize the majority, the fact that cries out to the reader is that human nature has got to change before the fine ideals for which the revolution was made can be realized. This is clearly a reversal of Marx and Engels, but it is a truth that has dogged every attempt to create socialist societies in our time. As Miller wrote: 'It is only by obeying our highest impulses that we can unite.' This contention is essentially the message of Koestler's work too: if we set out to create the perfect society through every volte-face and crime at our disposal, we shall only succeed in creating a nightmare-tyranny. To quote Miller again: 'The man with the gun, the man with murder in his heart, cannot possibly recognize Paradise even when he is shown it.'

Huxley's vision of the future raises, as we said, the problem of technological power, and the ends to which it is put by men – and I use terms which 'Abdu'l-Bahá used when referring to the discovery of nuclear power – men of inferior spirituality. Now it might appear more likely that modern man will destroy himself before he creates a brave new world – for the kind of shallow rationality we see personified in Huxley's Controller more often goes with a ruthless impulse to destroy. The missing ingredient in the book is that very savagery that civilized man with no moral core invariably possesses, and which Orwell and Koestler appreciate so well. But it is still conceivable that after a twentieth-century global catastrophe, a society bearing some of the features of Huxley's utopia may emerge from the ashes. What is the most frightening feature of this utopia is its Godlessness – its arrogant assumption of the powers of all lordship and control. This is the dream of twentieth-century man, and it is at the heart of his degradation. Indeed, all the utopias we have discussed, and this includes Miller's modern America, are built on a common materialism, a common denial of God, and a common belief in the all-sufficiency of man. Miller is also right in pointing out the banishment of the true artist from such societies. All great art glorifies both man and God. The twentieth century has not been a great one for the creations that nourish the soul; and surely artists are not vain in insisting that we remember our inner selves, that we nourish the faculty of vision. Otherwise where is our humanity? of what use is all our technological progress? For we have gained the world but lost our souls.

Through the minds of the great geniuses truths from the unseen world are made manifest; this is a process of renewal in every time, for the working of vision is always fresh and vital, like the workings of a child's mind. Henry Miller expresses the importance of the state of vision thus:

Back of every creation, supporting it like an arch, is faith. Enthusiasm is nothing: it comes and goes. But if one *believes*, then miracles occur. Faith has nothing to do with profits; if anything, it has to do with prophets. Men who know and believe can foresee the future. They don't want to put something over – they want to put something *under* us. They want to give solid support to our dreams. The world isn't kept running because it's a paying proposition. (God doesn't make a cent on the deal.) The world goes on because a few men in every generation believe in it utterly, accept it unquestioningly; they underwrite it with their lives. In the struggle which they have to make themselves understood they create music; taking the discordant elements of life, they weave a pattern of harmony and significance. If it weren't for this constant struggle on the part of a few creative types to expand the sense of reality in man the world *would* die out. We are not kept alive by legislators and militarists, that's fairly obvious. We are kept alive by men of faith, men of vision. They are like vital germs in the endless process of becoming. Make room, then, for the life-giving ones!

How difficult it is to convince the men of affairs, the 'practical men' who decide our destiny, of the reality of such things! Miller tells how Vivekananda went to America with such a mission, and was in the end driven to remonstrate with his audiences for their self-righteousness and lack of belief. Several years before the outbreak of the Great War in Europe, two orientals came to America. One was Rabindranath Tagore, the Bengali poet, and his reaction was the same as his compatriot's. The other was 'Abdu'l-Bahá 'Abbás, the Persian exile from Palestine. It is reported that his first remark upon viewing the skyscrapered skyline of Manhattan was: 'the minarets of the West'. This gentle irony can be perceived in his dealings with the materialist philosophers whom he likened to a herd of cows. His published talks reveal a patient wisdom, in their subtle use of natural metaphors to suggest the universal pattern behind the interdependent material and spiritual worlds.

'Abdu'l-Bahá's words give a new perspective to the twentieth century's despair before the failure of the utopian vision:

The Call of God, when raised, breathed a new life into the body of mankind, and infused a new spirit into the whole creation. *It is for this reason that the world hath been moved to its depths*, and the hearts and consciences of men been quickened. Ere long the evidences of this regeneration will be revealed, and the fast asleep will be awakened.

Could it be that there really is some balm for those alienated from these our times, for the masses, very soon to suffer the same disillusionment? The assurance that we may derive from 'Abdu'l-Bahá's prophecy that all is not lost, that on the contrary, all is yet to gain, must now be a matter of faith. But we have seen that faith is indeed the miracle required; a faith in the power of our inner vision and, ultimately, in the power of God. Such a power cannot let us down as have every one of our man-made creeds. Moreover, if we are to believe the words of 'Abdu'l-Bahá, a new spirit has been infused into the whole creation. We have not to turn to the exhausted spirit of past religious creeds, but to the transforming spirit which is the force of the new age itself.

For of the life-giving ones, of the men of vision, there is One Who is transcendent, and on Whose coming all others wait for their inspiration. This is the Promised Avatar, the One Who arises from Age to Age, when goodness dies out, and evil appears to prevail. Indeed, were it not for this Genius what a blighted planet this would be; what impenetrable darkness would cover the face of society, without hope of illumination. Thank God that it is not so.

The Bahá'í Faith and the Philosophy of History

> There is not only *Time*, but there are *times*, and
> succession of times, epoch after epoch, and age
> succeeding age.   *Johann Gottlieb Fichte*[1]

> Do you know in what Day you are living? Do you
> realize in what Dispensation you are alive?
> *'Abdu'l-Bahá*[2]

IT IS ONE of the tragedies of this age that the name of J. G. Fichte
echoes across the gulf of time to conjure up that of Adolf Hitler.
It is true that outside the Marxist world philosophies of history
are no longer fashionable. Yet if we are to answer 'Abdu'l-
Bahá's question and discover the meaning of the day in which
we live, we have again to turn to history and ask it to yield its
secrets. In spite of the totalitarian movements whose abuse of
truth has not only been in the field of history, we must reach
again beyond that purblind toying with superficial cause and
effect that has been the pursuit of too many twentieth–century
Western historians.

It is the view of the Bahá'í Faith that the modern age has a
precise and crucial meaning in the history of mankind. Such a
view sees our own times in the perspective of a distant future to
which they must give birth. So unprecedented is this present
epoch in the destiny of mankind that according to 'Abdu'l-Bahá
men shall look back and speak of the 'glorious twentieth century'!

1. J. G. Fichte, *Über das Wesen des Gelehrten*, trans. W. Smith, *Fichte's Popular Works*,
vol. I, London, 1889, p. 225.
2. From a talk in Paris, 1913, quoted in *Star of the West*, vol. IV, no. 6.

The Bahá'í writings on history, as in any other subject they treat of, interpret to man what he needs to know for his betterment and happiness. To the extent that the Bahá'í Faith discovers laws and meanings in history which when learnt will be to the enlightenment of man, it may be said to possess a philosophy of history. This philosophy is no philosopher's dream–castle, but of vital importance to an age that has lost its way. Its significance once apprised, humanity will be at the beginning of achieving the wonderful promise it holds out.

The Bahá'í Faith in Modern History

When looking at the teachings of the Bahá'í Faith, and its history, we see at once how rooted both are in the real conditions of the modern age. Not only is the Bahá'í Faith the newest independent historical religion; it is also impossible to evaluate either its message or its appeal without reference to the wider development of the modern world, with which it is inextricably linked.

The decade, even the year, from which the new faith traces its inauguration is of significance. The decade was the 1840s, one of peculiarly intense change in Europe, where political forces were arraying themselves for a showdown with the old order that in the year of revolutions 1848–9 was to disturb severely the kings of Europe. Religious doubt was making an appearance on a significant scale. Individuals like the young English intellectuals, A. H. Clough, John Sterling and James Anthony Froude, were agonizing over the Anglican faith; Chambers' *Vestiges of the Natural History of Creation* appeared, laying the foundations for the great battles between scientists and Christian clergy in the 1860s.

Great Britain was well advanced along the path of industrialization, but economic changes were afoot on the European continent too. It was the decade of the railways, and the telegraph sent its first message across the world on 23 May 1844.

It was at that moment that the new religion was born in

Persia. In fact the religion of Siyyid 'Alí-Muhammad, the merchant-Prophet of Shiraz (as he was to become known to Europeans), began also on 23 May when he announced his mission to his first follower in his native city. It was not very long before the new phenomenon was brought to the notice of the occident.[3] The Persians took to slaying their 'heretics' and in 1850 news reached Europe of the execution of the Báb (Gate); this was the title he had adopted.[4]

The Báb's brief charismatic career engendered permanent affection in the hearts of two Frenchmen, A.-L.-M. Nicolas and the Comte de Gobineau. Both saw the Bábí movement as a triumphant, meteor-like illumination of the darkened horizon of a once glorious people. Its apparent quenching by the vicious forces of religion and state only enhanced its glow. Neither they nor any other European of that epoch saw the cause of the Báb as the prelude to something far greater in scope. They heard the overture little knowing what was to follow.

The issue of the Báb's successor, it is fair to say, was in part responsible for this. That Bahá'u'lláh, previously an eminent Bábí, was not the Báb's successor but the greater one the Báb had foretold would come after him, was eventually accepted by all but a small minority of the Báb's followers. Bahá'u'lláh's personality transformed the Bábí movement, but European commentators were unable to get him in focus. Even E. G. Browne, whose pen-portrait of Bahá'u'lláh remains the most remarkable statement yet by a European upon the phenomenon of the new Faith, could not efface his preconceptions of the Báb in his estimation of what was now no longer the Bábí but the Bahá'í Faith.[5]

The Báb's address to his followers, which was made in the early summer of 1844 and recorded by Nabíl-i-A'zam, captures the millennial zeal which was a feature of so many movements and ideas of this decade. One sentence alone encapsulates what for many in various parts of the world had

3. See M. Momen, *The Bábí and Bahá'í Religions, 1844–1944*, pp. 3–5, 83–5.
4. See H. M. Balyuzi, *The Báb*, Appendix 7, pp. 217–24.
5. See H. M. Balyuzi, *Edward Granville Browne and the Bahá'í Faith*.

become a life-cause: 'You are the witnesses of the Dawn of the promised Day of God.' It could almost have been the language of one of the evangelical sects waiting at that time for the advent of the Lord. Many of their members were to die perplexed by the failure of scriptural prophecy to come true.

The Bábís fought their battles and espoused their leader's cause in the name of the *Ṣáḥibu'z-Zamán*, or Lord of the Age. Theirs was the consciousness of living in the Day of Resurrection, when the trumpet had been sounded and the one promised by Muhammad had appeared with a new revelation and a new book superseding the Koran. Beyond this was a promise of still greater things – no less than the advent of the Lord himself whom they knew from the Báb's writings as 'He Whom God will make manifest'. When Bahá'u'lláh claimed this station for himself he offered as proof a stream of writings proclaiming the dawn of a new day. 'The Day of God' became the mighty theme in hundreds of lines in his works. The central themes of Bahá'í belief became the appearance of the promised deliverer and the inauguration of the 'Day of God'.

Within the framework of their Islamic background, to the first Bábís and Bahá'ís their faith was in a wonderful, unfathomable way the cynosure of history. They conceived of history as a succession of revelations of the divinity; this latest was also the greatest, being the fulfilment of all others. From it would stem events and achievements that would transform the world into a paradise.

It was a similar dream to many of the political and religious millennialists of the epoch, only it had as its towering focus a religious figure who personified for his followers the entire aspiration. In Fichtean terms the Divine Idea of the age and the Divine Man had coalesced – for the scholar of religion that ever-miraculous and mystic event had occurred: one of the world's great religions, of which we know but a handful, had been born in the nineteenth century. Given the aspirations of the age as a whole – and we might remember scripture-searching evangelicals and messianic Saint-Simonian socialists as well as many others in this – it was apt. The spirit of the age had given birth to a movement of chiliastic significance. Expectancy had not been cheated, though few realized it; well might Jowett say later in the century: 'The Bahá'í Movement is the greatest light to come into the world since Jesus Christ.'

This religion, which had appeared in an age of millennialism, and gave to the world in the person of Bahá'u'lláh another of history's bestriding Messiahs, was to stand inextricably bound to the course of a century and more of extreme change in all spheres of human behaviour. Bahá'u'lláh went so far as to associate this change with his own coming: 'Soon', he wrote, 'will the present-day order be rolled up, and a new one spread out in its stead.'

From the beginning the new movement was neither archaic nor Janus-like. In its country of origin its followers were branded innovators and heretics. Ṭáhirih, the Iranian poetess and Bábí, openly defied the ceremonies of Shí'i Islam, disregarding the commemoration of the martyrdom of Ḥusayn in the month of Muḥarram, and eventually doing the unthinkable in publicly removing her veil. It was the symbolic act that ended the dispensation of Islam, and concretely identified the Bábí-Bahá'í movement with the most licentious principles in the eyes of orthodoxy. The emancipation of women had been launched in the East, nigh on eighty years before full female suffrage in the United Kingdom. The autocratic power of ecclesiastics was denied, and reactionary *mujtahids* and *mullas* castigated from their pulpits these heretical departures from Islam.

But the most visionary contribution of the Bahá'í Faith was yet to come. Bahá'u'lláh's writings of the 1860s and 70s, disseminated from his places of detention and imprisonment in the domains of the Ottomans, addressed the leaders of the world with the news of his prophethood and prophecies of the future. Unless these leaders combined to establish peace and root out social injustice, Bahá'u'lláh promised, their countries would be thrown into chaos, and their own exalted positions succumb to revolution. Such warnings possess an astounding veracity when we view the period in world history, 1870–1918.

When they had ignored his summons, Bahá'u'lláh wrote of a 'lesser peace' which could be established by the world's leaders in default of the 'Most Great Peace' that would have eventuated from their recognition of his station. At the same time he spoke of a 'new life' that was 'stirring in all the peoples of the world', but which none had properly recognized. This he associated with the coming unity of mankind, which would take the form of a world commonwealth of peoples. Few could visualize such a state: true, Enlightenment and early nineteenth-century idealist philosophers had spoken of a world federation, and Prince Albert referred to the unity of mankind at the Great Exhibition in London in 1851. Yet here was a prisoner of the Sultan of Turkey inviting the world's principalities to establish it. Was the bearer of such a message under a Fourier-like delusion, was he mad, or had he seen God sitting at the loom of time weaving? With the passing of Bahá'u'lláh in 1892, the faith he had founded was launched beyond the East, and proved the universality of its appeal by becoming established in the new world. The journey of Bahá'u'lláh's son and appointed successor, the unique 'Abdu'l-Bahá, first to Europe in 1911, then on to America in 1911–12, had immense implications for the history of religion. Neither St Peter nor St Paul had made a more portentous voyage than that which brought 'Abdu'l-Bahá to New York on 11 April 1912. His message, unlike that of the gurus and occultists who had begun to proselytize in Europe and North America in the 1880s, was no modernizing of ancient Hindu or esoteric philosophies – it was a call to men of goodwill everywhere to relinquish racial, religious and class prejudice, and establish a universal brotherhood and peace that was alone worthy of the modern age. It contrasted too with the narrow evangelism of the fundamentalist Christian sects as yet unwilling to yield their sense of superiority and separatism from the non-Christian traditions and cultures of mankind. Soured by their own failure to make any impact in these areas, evangelical missionaries accused 'Abdu'l-Bahá of pandering to the liberal theories of the West in order to make converts. It was a telling accusation: the promise of the Bahá'í teachings was now held up before the most progressive leaders of thought. Among those who came within its orbit were the eminent Swiss scientist and social philosopher, August Forel, and the great Tolstoy.

'Abdu'l-Bahá had gone to the western world to warn it of the consequences of materialism and creedal hatreds: the outbreak of the Great War in 1914 set the twentieth century on an irreversible course of destruction. In 1920 'Abdu'l-Bahá wrote privately, 'in the future another war, fiercer than the last, will assuredly break out'. The possibility of the Bahá'í message of peace mitigating the apocalyptic upheavals to follow was now very small indeed. 'The time for the destruction of the world and its people hath arrived', Bahá'u'lláh had earlier written.

It was in recognition that modern man collectively had failed to respond to the spirit of universalism that Shoghi Effendi, 'Abdu'l-Bahá's grandson and appointed successor, enunciated the Bahá'í view of contemporary history in his writings of the 1930s and 40s. His most stringent argument was that humanity was now gripped in the clutches of forces it could neither control nor understand. A tempest was 'sweeping the face of the earth', uprooting the foundations of every settled form of life. It was a divinely-ordained, retributive and cleansing force that was preparing mankind for 'that culminating and blissful stage in their long, their slow and painful evolution throughout the ages, which is at once their inalienable right and their true destiny'.[6] For the meantime, no pragmatic or idealistic states-manship could avail; insidious destructive forces, which he associated with the 'triple false gods' of 'racialism, nationalism and communism', were leading the world to imminent catastrophe.

Such a view did not qualify for a moment the Bahá'í vision of a glorious destiny for mankind, because the disruption itself was preparation. The unity of mankind was no 'pious hope', its implications were 'deeper, its claims greater than any which the Prophets of old were allowed to advance'. Rather, what would necessarily occur before this goal might be achieved, was 'the

6. *The Promised Day Is Come*, p. 3.

fire of a severe ordeal, unparalleled in its intensity', which could 'fuse and weld the discordant entities that constitute the elements of present-day civilization, into the integral components of the world commonwealth of the future'.[7]

According to Shoghi Effendi, the age of transition was still with us. The old world order was being rolled up – but from where would come the new? The ultimate claim of the Bahá'í Faith was that the Bahá'í community itself, destined to embrace the majority of mankind, constituted the new order, the order conceived by its Prophet, that must replace the old. Founded on Bahá'u'lláh's teachings, the Bahá'í community was the incubus of a future civilization. As the Christian and Muslim communities before, it had the power, a far greater power than they, to triumph over the decaying order around it, and emerge upholding the banner of human values.

At the time of Shoghi Effendi's passing, the foundations for such an astounding global strategy were being laid. The history of the spread of the Bahá'í Faith within the one hundred and thirty and more years of its existence is another subject which cannot be written here.

The Bahá'í View founded on Revelation

Few historians dare make prophetic statements about the future; such an activity is held to be unscientific. Prophets are fortunately not tied to the craft of professional historian, yet it is fair to remark that if anyone embarks upon the field of prophecy his failures should be recorded alongside what he gets right. It is thus that historians rarely feel threatened by the prophecies of journalists, visionaries and astrologers. The random truths in the sayings of such do not warrant their being accorded consistent respect.

When Jesus looked down upon the Temple and said not a stone would be left standing on another, it wanted some forty years before his words came true. Biblical scholars intent upon

7. Shoghi Effendi, 'The Goal of a New World Order', in *The World Order of Bahá'u'lláh*, pp. 43, 46.

unravelling the prophecies in the last century often had the feeling that the same was at last coming to pass with respect to the twenty-fourth chapter of St Matthew. The central figures in the Bahá'í Faith were as equally categorical as Christ. Bahá'u'lláh promised the fall of the empire of the French Emperor, Louis Napoleon, a year before the débâcle at Sedan. In the 1870s he forecast the 'lamentation' of Berlin, though at that point her 'conspicuous glory' was in the creation of a second German Reich and her hegemony over France. Bahá'u'lláh saw the banks of the Rhine 'covered with gore', an event that would occur a second time. 'Abdu'l-Bahá prophesied in 1920 'another war, fiercer than the last'. Shoghi Effendi wrote of a 'world catastrophe' in 1933. Nor can we find any example of a statement by any of these figures of an event or innovation which did not occur when they said it would; yet they were so categorical. The French agent in Akka who transmitted Bahá'u'lláh's prophecy to the French Emperor in 1869 had no doubts of the authority of him who sent it when he received news of Louis Napoleon's fate a year later.

It is certainly too late to hope to convince western scientists and intellectuals that data received by the senses and analysed by the rational mind are neither sufficient on their own to arrive at truth, nor the only means of knowledge at man's disposal. Yet we have to admit that the pronouncements of the figures of the Bahá'í Faith are not ultimately based on research and analysis of such a kind. Given the confinement and harassment they suffered during their lives such an approach would not have been practicable. 'Abdu'l-Bahá spoke of the inspiration of the Holy Spirit as the only sure means of arriving at truth. How can such a source be verifed? – we simply have to look at the evidence of the writings of these figures, and the incidence of how often what they said came to pass. Of course, we are not bidden discard our criteria of reason in judging what they have said, since in the Bahá'í teaching revelation cannot disagree with reason.

The Bahá'í teachings present an interpretation of history that is confessedly *a priori*: 'Abdu'l-Bahá's explanations of the nature of existence proceed from an intuitive, not empirical knowledge in the first instance. His sources, beyond the scope of his own conversance with classical history and philosophy, rested upon the knowledge and inspiration he derived from his father, Bahá'u'lláh. Shoghi Effendi likewise obtained his inspiration from Bahá'u'lláh and 'Abdu'l-Bahá. As a religion, the Bahá'í Faith speaks not only to the intellectual part of man but to the spiritual, and the Bahá'í understanding of history is likewise based on the assurance that this world has a creator and a vivifier: that all things begin and end in God, and all knowledge emanates from him.

Religious Views of History

Having said that the Bahá'í view of history derives from criteria established by revelation, that it has its beginning and end in faith in God, and that it is concerned not only with the intellectual but with the spiritual in man, it becomes self-evident that its view of history is religious. Yet here we must tread carefully, because the Bahá'í concept of revelation may in practice be unlike, for instance, the Christian view; and providential control of history may be understood in a different sense in respect of its workings than in Christianity or Islam. We shall be more precise in our discussion of the Bahá'í concept of God's role in history, so we must bear in mind from the beginning that the term 'providential' may not here hold the specialized meaning given it by earlier writers on ideas of history, who have in mind the providential aspect of the Christian view of history.

Not all higher religions possess a profound interest in history. With all respect to the Hindu epics, it cannot be maintained that they have anything particular to tell us about a Hindu philosophy of history. If Hindu philosophy can be said to include within it a philosophy of history, it would consist of the discussion of one aspect of the timeless, unchanging, transcendent reality which is held to underlie all things. In practice, Hinduism has taken next to no interest in the writing of history. The same might be said of Buddhism which has an even more ahistorical outlook in its pessimistic appraisal of human activity.

Jewish history in its relation to religion possesses a greater significance. It is first of all in Judaism that a regard for literal historic occurrence acquires such a great religious importance. That God revealed himself to Moses upon Mount Sinai upon a given occasion becomes of untold significance, and its actual occurrence as recorded in scripture is an article of faith. Alongside this went the universalist view of the later prophets of Israel, holding all men equal before God's judgement seat: the idea of God the judge, punisher and rewarder of men in history.

This concern for God's historical dealings with mankind was bequeathed to the Semitic daughter religions, Christianity and Islam. The belief that God's testimony to men is to be found in actual historical events, recorded in scripture, is to be observed in the New Testament tradition and in the Koran. Christianity and Islam, therefore, both make the claim to be historically founded. 'Christianity is a historical religion', writes a recent evangelist. 'It claims that God has taken the risk of involving himself in human history, and the facts are there for you to examine with the utmost rigour.'[8] Modern Christians point to the New Testament, not in a spirit of defence but with aggressive challenge to disprove the Gospel record.

Islam has an even clearer claim to be a historical religion since the life of its founder is accredited by all sources and the astoundingly successful spread of its system is one of the most remarkable phenomena of history.

Both faiths possess a schematic view of history. The Christian view has been called 'apocalyptic', that is, it sees history as a division in two: the first period being one of darkness, the second one of light. The outstanding event that marks the division is the Incarnation, in which God enters history in person through Jesus Christ. The Old Testament is the record of God's preparation of man for this event and can be

8. Michael Green, *Man Alive!*, London, 1967, p. 61.

categorized as 'epoch-making', that is a subdividing of events not as important as the Incarnation but still held to be relevant.[9] The uniqueness of the Incarnation throws an overwhelming importance on the few years of Christ's earthly ministry; the whole of human history is seen to lead up to and away from this unique divine intervention. The stark apocalyptic view of history subsists in the belief in *providential* control of history: Christianity attributes the power to cause events to God; man has really no volition of his own and is just an agent. Future development is foreseen in the expectancy of a 'Last Day', when human history will be suddenly ended by the Divinity, causing tremendous upheavals on earth and in the heavens. Following this a new heaven and a new earth will appear; it is to be stressed that in these events man is to have no part – all will be effected by God. This prophetic view is termed 'eschatological' and represents the most arbitrary part of the Christian schema, for while there was historical evidence to support the theory of Incarnation, the eschatological prognosis rests upon none at all.

That God's involvement in human history should be called a 'risk' suggests the marked disinterest Christianity has had in large areas of history. There is the suggestion that God does not care about a great deal that man does – that darkness and ignorance have been allowed control and God has absented himself. Man is given innately the power only to perform evil. God could rescue him if he wished by infusing his grace, but with the exception of his elect, he chooses to leave the majority of mankind to its evil devices.

The Christian view of providential involvement in history is thus highly arbitrary. 'The work of providence in history is recognized, but recognized in a way which leaves nothing for man to do.'[10] In addition, it seems the non-Christian is merely so much waste-product; from Augustine to Calvin, the following holds true: 'the whole movement of history has the purpose of securing the happiness of a small portion of the

9. These categories are to be found in R. G. Collingwood, *The Idea of History*, part II, pp. 1–3.
10. ibid. p. 55.

human race in another world; it does not postulate a further development of human history on earth'.[11] This world is but a vale of tears from which only the elect emerge with success.

Islam, coming after Christianity, endorsed belief in God's intervention in history through Christ, but flatly repudiating any notion of anthropomorphism, and denying the uniqueness of Jesus, discarded the Christian apocalyptic view of history. Instead it offered a more embracing view, but one still founded on the idea of a succession of divine interventions in history. God had revealed his purpose to men through a succession of messengers, to different groups of men at different times. Not only Jesus, but Moses, Abraham, Noah, and sundry Arabian prophets brought God's word to men. Muhammad was 'the seal of the prophets', the last of the line. At first view it appears that Islam has greatly broadened the Jewish idea of God's historical covenant, establishing his testimony not at one point in time and to one people, but to a whole group of peoples who were recipients of their own prophets. God's continuing revelation to man in history was attested by the Koran, which was the perfection of God's word to all men.

Yet for all its universalism, Islam adopted a similar fundamentalism to Judaism and Christianity. Muhammad was the last prophet, therefore it followed that revelation was at an end, the Koran was the final intervention of God's providence. Islam thus became as doctrinaire in its view of history succeeding its prophet as Christianity in its attitude toward events after Christ. Though it held less contempt for the field of human activity, endeavouring with its theocratic claim to complete divine control over human society through the Islamic community, Islam too found itself looking backwards in time to an event that stamped a finality upon history. God's intervention in history was complete, its repository was the Koran, its custodian the Islamic community. All that remained was a similar denouement to history as we find in the Christian eschatology with the Last Day. Moreover, according to orthodoxy, providential control over human destiny, and thus human history,

11. J. B. Bury, *The Idea of Progress*, p. 21.

gave no more space for man's volition than did Christianity.

It will be seen how in the Bahá'í understanding of history some of the traditional religious modes of viewing it are differently stressed, if not substantially altered and re-orientated. What interests us at present is to see how these traditional world-pictures were challenged and effectively driven from the field by humanistic developments in thought.

The Advent of Humanism

With the passing of the medieval-Christian world-picture, Renaissance philosophers began to conceive of man as the measure of his own world. The traditional idea of history was not immediately vanquished, for the power of the Church was still strong, and thinkers like Erasmus and Francis Bacon chose not to alienate religion. Bacon's innovations were in the natural sciences, and it was here that his concentration on 'secondary causes' as opposed to the intrusive attribution of every question to a divine providence, opened the way to rational inquiry in other spheres. However, if the sphere of knowledge governed by the natural sciences at first appeared innocuous, change came very quickly. The natural sciences became such a pre-occupation that the way of looking at the natural world spread to the domain of man himself. For a while history was treated as an extension of the natural sciences; laws were sought that could provide the same rational explanations for historical events and developments as the laws held to operate in the natural world. Natural law became as authoritarian a controlling factor in philosophies of history in the eighteenth century as Providence had been in the middle ages.

However, history was now highly regarded in itself; the eighteenth century 'was . . . an age of consuming interest in history. History was a craft, a discipline, and an enter-tainment.'[12] It also was an important element in the burgeoning struggle between anti-Christian humanists and orthodox Christians. The *philosophe* wished to take control of history:

12. P. Gay, *The Enlightenment: An Interpretation*, vol. II, *The Science of Freedom*, p. 369.

once man had grasped the laws of social behaviour, he said, he could then control his own history. Bending these laws to his own will, man might create the perfect society hitherto dreamt of only by seers.

Here was a vital difference between orthodox religion and humanistic, secular thinkers: the latter had already discarded original sin with its incapacitating influence on aspirations for improving man's lot. Instead they held optimistic ideas on human perfectibility that were scandalously blasphemous in the eyes of churchmen. The latter saw such ideas as a threat to the sway of the Church, and as the churches mainly stood associated with the present social order, the battle of ideas covered the struggle between change and social conservatism, democracy and absolutism.

The Romantic epoch sought to redress the atheism implicit across the spectrum of Enlightenment thought. Romantic philosophers like Schiller and Schlegel saw history as the second volume of God's revelation after the 'book of Nature'. They rediscovered the imaginative wonder of history, opening great vistas into the past, suggesting the universal importance of history, its unfathomable depths, and the uniqueness of each age. The Enlightenment had effectively only reversed the Christian apocalypse of light and darkness, making instead the age of Antiquity one of enlightenment and the Christian middle ages a time of barbarism. In the writings of Herder the variety and individuality of earlier cultures, including the non-European, was vindicated. Romanticism rescued whole areas of the past from the curse of prejudice, both Enlightenment and European ethnocentric.

At the very end of the eighteenth century, Immanuel Kant wrote thus:

The history of the human race, viewed as a whole, may be regarded as the realization of a hidden plan of nature to bring about a political constitution, internally, and, for this purpose, also externally perfect, as the only state in which all the capacities implanted by her in mankind can be fully developed.[13]

13. See *Theories of History*, ed. P. Gardener, p. 30.

Such a plan would yield, only after 'revolutions and transformations', 'a universal cosmopolitical institution'. The usually wary philosopher was expressing an idea common to both Enlightenment and Romantic thinkers: the idea of progress toward a superior world-society. The optimism of philosophers was reflected to a greater extent in the millenarian movements and sects that proliferated around the turn of the century and went on growing through the first half of the new one. History was suddenly taken over by prophets who claimed to read the entire significance of history in the light of a coming millennium. It seemed that never before had men's actions been so governed by a sense of their living through the fruition of great historical forces.

The idea of progress was soon to be found ubiquitously: in the vast mystic schemes of history conceived by Fichte, the socialistic theories of Saint-Simon and Robert Owen, the technocratic ideal of Jeremy Bentham, and the libertarian creed of William Godwin. It was an idea that became a faith, indulged in by idealist and materialist alike – hard-headed iron manufacturer and visionary reformer. The idea of progress, the faith in a better world, eventually became a commonplace, and taken up by the proponents of Britain's industrial might it became a shallow cliché that masked insensitivity and greed.

One section of Western society remained unimpressed: for orthodox Christians there was no secular 'goal of history'; outside the Church which was the custodian of the redemptive power of Jesus Christ, there was no salvation – Christ alone was the meaning of history. The Bible contained all the history Christians needed to know; to adopt the ideas of liberal secular thinkers was nothing less than infidelity.

Theories of progress could be left to secularists and prophets of socialism, but the advance of science was another matter. It was palpable, it could be seen –, an invention like the railway changed entire patterns of life. The belief in progress could not but be associated with the expansion of scientific discovery. Herein was the threat to the Church: the discovery of ever more laws in the natural sciences, and the confidence that science would find the means to the perfection of human society, seemed to lead to inevitable conflict with the static ideas of the Christian establishment. Renan spoke for many intellectuals when, writing in 1848, he phrased the matter thus:

> We have now come to a point at which we must choose between two faiths. If we despair of reason, we may find a refuge from utter scepticism in a belief in the external authority of the Roman Church. If we trust reason, we must accept the march of the human mind and justify the modern spirit.[14]

The debate over evolution crystallized the matter: 'Man appeared to owe his origin to the operation of impersonal and natural forces or laws instead of to the direct, personal action of a God.'[15] Though evolutionary theory had questionable implications for the idea of progress, it became the common cry among secularists that Darwin had disproved the Bible.

The advance of secularism thus accompanied the growth of science. Well into the twentieth century the belief was current that science and progress were synonymous. With the defeat of religious orthodoxy went the discarding of the Christian view of history, to be replaced by secular philosophies of history.

The failure of orthodox religion to meet the challenge of the shaping ideas of the modern era – scientific theory, evolution, rationalism and the faith in progress – must be accounted one of its most signal failures. If spiritually the churches were already forfeiting control over the laity owing to their complaisance in an antiquated and unjust social order, intellectually they never faced up to the fundamental factors at work in the formation of modern society. For Christendom the results were catastrophic: losing the battle for men's minds, the Christian churches saw secular power submerge their social role and effectively diminish their relevance in the making of modern history. For society as a whole these effects might be considered equally disastrous: discarding the belief in providential control of history, it adopted humanistic philosophies that placed the criteria for behaviour solely upon man's

14. J. B. Bury, *The Idea of Progress*, p. 321.
15. A. R. Vidler, *The Church in an Age of Revolution*, p. 117.

conception of utility. Science came under the guidance of mere rationalistic utilitarianism; while within society the decline of religion weakened moral sanctions and encouraged individual irresponsibility.

Was this inevitable? Was it impossible to embrace the new scientific spirit and the aspirations for the improvement of society without yielding up assurance of providential involvement in history? If man had truly outgrown the ideas of Providence represented in the old religions, whence was to come a new conceptualization of this power, suited to the scientific spirit of the new age?

The Bahá'í View of Providence and Progress

At first sight it is evident that the Bahá'í view of history combines both a providential and a humanistic approach to history. On the one hand, God is acclaimed the Lord of History; on the other, man is held to be the apogee of creation, the sole reason for life in the universe, and therefore in his history is to be found the meaning for the creation itself.

The Bahá'í view of history, as of nature, is teleological. 'Abdu'l-Bahá states that the natural world is under the complete control of God 'and is not a fortuitous composition and arrangement'. Man is the apogee of creation, for: 'If man did not exist, the universe would be without result, for the object of existence is the appearance of the perfections of God.' Man is 'the centre where the glory of all the perfections of God shine forth'.[16]

The earth appeared through a process of evolution, and though man was not there at the beginning, his existence was potential: 'In the womb of the world mind and spirit also existed in the embryo, but they were concealed; afterward they appeared.' The entire creation was from the beginning subject to a plan, which, however, evolved according to law: 'All beings, whether large or small, were created perfect and complete from the first, but their perfections appear in them by

16. *Some Answered Questions*, p. 196.

degrees. The organization of God is one; the evolution of existence is one; the divine system is one.'[17]

The creation of the universe was therefore for man: 'the human spirit is a Divine Trust, and it must traverse all conditions'. The purpose of life in this world is for the human spirit to acquire perfections: 'its passage and movement through the conditions of existence will be the means of its acquiring perfections'.[18] The history of mankind must therefore consist of his evolution towards perfection as a species, and as we are told perfections are endless, the existence of man must therefore be without end.

The observations that could be made concerning such a scheme are these: such a view might be endorsed by scientific discovery, but it is obviously an *a priori* system. It endorses and is of a kind with the statements of Genesis I. i: 'In the beginning God created the heaven and the earth'; and I. xxvi: 'And God said, Let us make man in our image, after our likeness . . .' The statements of revelation, according to Bahá'í belief, are the words of God, but they cannot disagree with the truths of science. It is clear also that the Bahá'í view of creation implies the development of life through a process of evolution according to natural law; man, however, always existed potentially as a separate and distinct species, not as an offshoot of a different species. Evolution according to Bahá'í teaching has a pre-ordained goal – in the scheme of evolution man is not a chance appearance! – the whole of evolution only makes sense with the appearance of the full perfections of man: 'if the perfections of the spirit did not appear in this world, this world would be unenlightened and absolutely brutal'.[19]

How then does man evolve? It follows from the above that man's progress is slow and accomplished by degrees. Lessing argued[20] that man's development involved an evolution collectively the same as in individual man. In the early stages

17. *Some Answered Questions* pp. 198–9.
18. ibid. p. 200.
19. ibid. p. 201.
20. In *The Education of the Human Race*, trans. W. B. Rönnfeldt, *The Laocoon and other Prose Writings*.

man was like a child; his religion treated him as such, educating him through threats, prohibitions and promises of reward. As he grew mature, his reason outgrew such teaching. As Lessing wrote: '. . . it will certainly come, the time of consummation, when man, however firmly his mind is convinced of an ever better future, will yet have no need to borrow motives for his conduct from the future. For he will do what is right because it is right, and not because arbitrary rewards are attached to it . . .'[21]

The argument adduced here for stages in human development is implicitly endorsed by 'Abdu'l-Bahá's analogy of the stages of growth to perfection:

The beginning of the existence of man on the terrestrial globe resembles his formation in the womb of the mother. The embryo in the womb of the mother gradually grows and develops until birth, after which it continues to grow and develop until it reaches the age of discretion and maturity. Though in infancy the signs of the mind and spirit appear in man, they do not reach the degree of perfection; they are imperfect. Only when man attains to maturity do the mind and the spirit appear and become evident in utmost perfection.[22]

This explains the patent imperfections in previous human history — these savour of the waywardness, passion and violence of childhood and adolescence. However, the seed of perfection was potentially present from the outset in man, and where he chose to utilize his inborn potential he did, as Herder suggests, improve his condition:

Were [man] contented with his condition, or were the means of his improvement not yet ripened in the ample field of time; he remained for ages what he was, and became nothing more. But if he employed the instruments God had given him for his use, his understanding, power, and all the opportunities that a favourable current conveyed to him; he raised himself higher with art, and improved himself with courage.[23]

'Abdu'l-Bahá explains that it was in the nature of man to

21. ibid. p. 287.
22. *Some Answered Questions*, p. 198.
23. J. G. Herder, *Ideen zur Philosophie der Geschichte der Menschheit*. Eng. trans. abr. F. E. Manuel, *Reflections on the Philosophy of The History of Mankind*, p. 107.

progress: '. . . gradually he made progress in perfectness, and grew and developed until he reached the state of maturity, when the mind and the spirit became visible in the greatest power.' The process of the manifestation of these qualities of maturity was necessarily slow and by degrees: 'The seed does not at once become a tree, the embryo does not at once become a man . . . No, they grow and develop gradually and attain the limit of perfection.'[24]

Human history thus expresses an organic development; one stage is not belittled as compared with another, as each had its part in the overall unfoldment. 'One day teaches another, one century instructs another century: tradition is enriched: the muse of Time, History, herself sings with a hundred tongues, speaks with a thousand tongues.'[25]

Man therefore has the potential to progress by virtue of the human spirit, or 'rational soul', as 'Abdu'l-Bahá terms it: 'In this perception and in this power all men are sharers . . . This human rational soul is God's creation . . . All sciences, knowledge, arts, wonders, institutions, discoveries and enterprises come from the exercised intelligence of the rational soul.'[26] Wherever he utilizes his innate powers to the full, man progresses. History is a record of mankind's slow development towards maturity.

The Bahá'í view, however, is not as deterministic (as we find is Herder's and other philosophers of history) as to suggest that man can reach perfection unaided, solely by means of the faculties implanted by the creator – or if he could, it would take an unconscionable time. History shows how all too frequently civilization is quenched, either through its own decadence or through the force of an outside agent; then dark ages are observed. A further *leitmotif* is required to move man other than the dynamic of the rational soul. It is here that the Bahá'í teachings insist on further intervention by Providence: the providential plan is operative not only from the setting into

24. *Some Answered Questions*, p. 199.
25. Herder, op. cit.
26. *Some Answered Questions*, p. 217.

motion of the process of evolution. There is providential intervention within the process of historical evolution itself; for the human spirit is otherwise insufficient to carry forward this scheme in anything but the most painfully retarded way.

God intervenes in history – we should say he guides the ultimate course of history – by revealing his will through messengers, or 'Manifestations', who are his representatives and mediators to man. These Manifestations possess an altogether higher power than the limited power of the rational soul. Their power is universal and born of the Divinity:

This universal mind is divine; it embraces existing realities, and it receives the light of the mysteries of God. It is a conscious power, not a power of investigation and of research. The intellectual power of the world of nature is a power of investigation . . . but the heavenly intellectual power, which is beyond nature, embraces things and is cognizant of things . . . This divine intellectual power is the special attribute of the Holy Manifestations.[27]

It is in fact for the purpose of the moral and intellectual training of man, and for his spiritual awakening that these 'Divine Educators' appear. Without a Jesus, a Moses, a Muhammad the record of human civilization would surely be greatly the worse. Left without their civilizing, morally elevating influence, where would man be now? Education, 'Abdu'l-Bahá says, is of three kinds: material, human and spiritual. The first deals with the body; the second with 'civilization and progress'; divine education is concerned with heavenly perfections and is 'the goal of the world of humanity'.[28] Whilst undoubtedly great souls appear in history who fulfil one or more of these roles as educator, it is the Divine Manifestations who with intuitive knowledge and transcendent power cause the great advances in civilization through reorganizing man in society and revivifying his soul.

Bahá'u'lláh taught that it was the Manifestations of God who delivered man progressively from darkness to light, from barbarism to culture. 'Abdu'l-Bahá would underscore this

27. ibid. p 218.
28. ibid. p. 8.

truth by demonstrating the advance in morals and civilization brought about by each messenger. Christ 'brought to humanity the glad tidings of universal peace, and spread abroad teachings which were not for Israel alone but were for the general happiness of the whole human race'.[29] Muhammad raised the Arab tribes who 'were in the lowest depths of savagery and barbarism' to become 'superior to the other nations of the earth in learning, in the arts, mathematics, civilization, government, and other sciences'.[30] Bahá'u'lláh stated that although materialists did not accept the transcendental certitude of such holy figures, they did at least bear testimony to the purity and integrity of their lives. Not only in the great civilizations founded on their word, but in the sacrificial lives led by hundreds of thousands of their followers through history, we may say the Divine Manifestations have left an indelible imprint upon time.

The Bahá'í concept of progressive revelation establishes the major pattern of history to consist of the advent of these Manifestations of God, and the advance in civilization their appearance invokes. Their knowledge is all–embracing but the revelations they bring are always suited to the capacities of their hearers. Such revelations synchronize with new stages in human development. The Divine Educator is in fact the inaugurator of each stage. The Bahá'í view of providential involvement in this wise in human history can be called apocalyptic, but it represents a far wider understanding of apocalyptic periods than the Semitic faiths where revelation is either unique or final. The Bahá'í teachings state that such a scheme of providential activity is never-ending. History will never cease to record the appearance of God's Messengers.

It has been demonstrated now, how in the Bahá'í understanding of history, progress is not only the law, it is also the prerogative of the divine ordering of history. Progress is established by the aspiration to perfection implanted in the human spirit, and is assured by the motivating force the

29. *Some Answered Questions* p. 16.
30. ibid. pp. 18, 23.

Manifestations of God bring to bear upon history. In both these aspects it is the divine will that has so arranged matters – a will that operates through natural law, and through outside entry of revelation. And as man evolves so does religion. Great changes in the organization and thought of mankind more or less accompany a new dispensation in religion. It is as though a new springtime occurs periodically in history: 'Abdu'l-Bahá likened the appearance of the Divine Manifestation to the opening of a new seasonal cycle, with the winter of defunct practices and beliefs giving way to a renewal of inspiration in all the affairs of man.

> Ring out a slowly dying cause,
>   And ancient forms of party strife;
>   Ring in the nobler modes of life,
> With sweeter manners, purer laws.
>
> Ring in the valiant man and free,
>   The larger heart, the kindlier hand;
>   Ring out the darkness of the land,
> Ring in the Christ that is to be.

The Bahá'í philosophy of history, which has as its cornerstone a belief in progress through providential control of the historical process, thus represents a profound departure from previous providential views of history. Bahá'u'lláh has said: 'All men have been created to carry forward an ever-advancing civilization' – this assurance dispels the historical pessimism and *contemptus mundi* of the old religions, and extends to mankind immense hope and confidence for the future. A 'blissful' consummation to man's evolution, as we shall see, yet awaits him. Such, to use again the words of Shoghi Effendi, 'is [mankind's] inalienable right and their true destiny.'

Choice or Inevitability?

The problem with teleological schemes of history, religious or humanistic, is that in practice they seem to offer little scope for human volition – history is determined by forces or laws that are too big to opt out of; all man can do is bring himself in line with them, and if he does not it makes no difference because they will work themselves out anyway. Providence or 'laws of history' order history without human beings having any say in the matter. Isaiah Berlin spoke of this mode of viewing history – the 'teleological category' – as one where 'everything that seems useless, discordant, mean, ugly, vicious, distorted, is needed, if we but knew it, for the harmony of the whole which only the Creator of the world, or the world itself (if it could become wholly aware of itself and its goals), can know'.[31]

To say that Providence rules history is very fine – but what of the misery and suffering evident in so much of it? Looking at the record of civilization and of religion we might be sceptical as to the efficacy of Divine Providence. How was Christ's message of love and truth capable of turning into an Inquisition, and why was this allowed? Why have the benefits of the Zoroastrian, Jewish and Muslim faiths apparently been overtaken by the religious animosity between their followers?

The field of history is the field of conflict: truth is trodden in the dust before the forces of denial are put to flight and the true achieves its epiphany. Nor is this an end, because within time truth is in turn distorted until it is rendered virtually malevolent. This is particularly the case with religion, which always meets fierce opposition when it appears fresh and untainted in the world, but eventually passes through the stages of acceptance and beneficence until it decays and becomes a bar to progress. The reason for the successive appearance of the Manifestations is that truth is eventually lost amidst dogma, and the spirit of love and amity disappears and requires renewal. Man might see from history how often the majority persecute the small band of faithful: so much of human suffering is due to perversity. And if men chose to ignore the philosophers of morals and the prophets of science, whose fault was it but their own? If man is given the opportunity to accept truth and to progress, and yet rejects it, it must be allowed that he has choice, and that the responsibility for most that is ugly,

31. Isaiah Berlin, 'Historical Inevitability', repr. Patrick Gardener (ed.), *The Philosophy of History*, p. 164.

mean, and distorted, is his alone.

Acceptance of this is a sobering thought; it means that God has given man free choice, and he is not treated like an automaton. The fatalism that has crept into previous providential schemes of history is not a little due to the wish to absolve man of his power to choose and the responsibility this places upon him. 'I am like a jaded camel', the poet Rúmí cries, 'the saddle of free-will has sorely bruised my back . . . Let the ill-balanced load drop from me . . .'

While God has control of the course of history, man is not merely a puppet without the capacity to choose. All that he needs is given him to progress, but it is his free-will that has brought apparent chaos into the world. Moreover, the world is a testing field – the Prophet Muhammad said it was not enough to accept the truth, then one had to be tested in the fortitude with which he adhered to it. If man accepts the divine will, which is no *fiat* but the practical course to progress, all his powers are activated. It is his turning away that brings about the greatest suffering. But the timing of providential intervention which is the force that saves man from himself, remains inscrutable. So does providential 'punishment' – for in practice this means the leaving of man to his own cruel devices.

The question, too, as to how man can have free will and yet history be under providential predestination, defies human explanation. Such matters as the origin and destiny of man, his nature and his dependence on the Manifestations of God, and the ultimate control of history by Providence, are fixed by the Bahá'í teachings. Man's moral accountability is stressed as well, for the Bahá'í view of life, being profoundly ethical, does not explain away man's behaviour by attributing it to influences beyond his control. Yet the matter of free will and predestination, or, as Tolstoy posed it, that of choice in the individual and inevitability within the process of history, is a matter that will always cause bafflement. Too curiously pursued, it caused insanity, according to 'Alí Ibn Abú Ţalib, the first Imám.

Thus while the Bahá'í view of history is teleological,

discerning a pre-ordained goal to history and features of its movement, it in no way countenances the kind of deterministic thinking that absolves men from moral responsibility or the freedom to choose. If it did, it would make religious teaching nonsense. On the contrary, the Bahá'í view insists that man's purpose individually and collectively is to know and love God. This can only be achieved through volition: the improvement of life and the advance of man depend upon the struggle of the individual soul to improve itself. The whole of history waits upon that – according to the Bahá'í teachings God is neither authoritarian nor arbitrary. Assuredly, man has his part to play, and the readiness and intelligence with which he plays it affects his happiness and progress.

The Monist View of History

We saw how humanist theories of history arose in opposition to the pessimistic view of man taught by orthodox religion. Such a school as the mid-nineteenth-century Left-Hegelians in Germany had this reason for denying the existence of God, and calling him instead a projection of man's own nature in the creation of which man accomplished his 'self-alienation'. Their aim was to rescue man from the wretched, dualist picture of him in religion – hopelessly torn between his fallen sinful nature and the remnants of his divine descent. In freeing man from religion the humanists had the laudable aim of wishing to restore to him his self-respect, to make him whole and not divided. They sought to free him from religious 'myth' and make him, not God, the architect of his destiny. The concluding sentence from Feuerbach's Lectures on '*Das Wesen der Religion*' states the lectures are intended to change the hearers 'from friends of God to friends of man, from believers to thinkers, from men of prayer to workers, from candidates for the other world to students of this world, from Christians, who, by their own confession and admission, are "*half angels and half beasts*", to *men*, to *complete men*.'[32]

32. Quoted in H. Gollwitzer, *The Christian Faith and the Marxist Criticism of Religion*, Edinburgh, 1970, p. 52, n. 15.

Given the decadence of the old order, of which the Christian picture of a sinful mankind was an integral part, such views were of their time salutary. It was in the hands of Marx that Hegel's conceptualization of historical progress, and the atheism of the Left-Hegelians, were wedded to an economic theory of historical and social change, and became the most successful monist philosophy of history of the modern age.

The appeal of such an atheistic, monist philosophy is partly that it claims to free mankind from the opiate of religion. What were the undesirable features of this opiate? – it took man as divided and weak; it supported an absolutist and unjust social order; and therefore rejected the possibility of progress. Indeed, mankind would be better without that kind of religion. But we have shown that a belief in God can also accompany a belief in historical progress; that religion can in fact include humanistic elements. Moreover, the atheist view of man, endeavouring to take man whole, has not been able to reduce the brutality and greed within him. And by establishing a materialist, determinist philosophy of history like Marxism, it has actually minimized rather than expanded the freedom to choose. For this scheme of history is a good example of Isaiah Berlin's 'teleological category', in which individual choice is obviated and man has to yield to impersonal laws of history.

In contrast, the Bahá'í teachings see man as a composite being. He is neither the crudely dual creature of Christianity, nor the whole personality of the humanists – indeed, modern psychology has already disposed of that picture. Man is at the apex of the animal world and yet is at the beginning of the spiritual world: 'he is the end of imperfection and the beginning of perfection . . . He has the animal side as well as the angelic side'. Man is not strictly either – but it is obviously preferable that he advance in spirituality rather than animality. 'If he comes under the shadow of the True Educator and is rightly trained, he becomes . . . the source of spiritual qualities . . .'[33]

The Bahá'í view of man is therefore that his nature can be changed – he requires education both in intellect and in morals.

33. 'Abdu'l-Bahá, *Some Answered Questions*, pp. 235–6.

Man must be informed of spiritual truths if he is to progress; if we deny the spiritual nature of man – as atheism does theoretically – we are left with the same brutal man we know from the wars of history. To withhold man from the teachings of true religion is to take away his hopes of fundamental progress.

The monist view of history is therefore truncated in its exclusion of Providence, and simplistic because it ignores the composite character of man. It grew up as an attempt to release man from his chains but succeeded in making him a thrall to an impersonal historical process. It purports to change man through his environment, but never getting to the essence of man's nature still finds him the same limited creature as of old.

It is clear from the writings of Bahá'u'lláh and 'Abdu'l-Bahá that man is primarily a spiritual being, and that only through the exercise of his spiritual faculties can a harmonious and beneficial world be created. This is to be achieved through a partnership between God and man through which civilization is advanced rationally and materially at the same time as it is founded upon the deepest principles of metaphysical truth. In this way it becomes both divinely ordered and humanistic in its achievement. The faculties of the human spirit are willingly trained by the Divine Educator, the Manifestation of God, whose religious system is a protective umbrella for every soul.

The Goal of History

We have seen that the purpose of man's existence as a species is to develop towards maturity, and the state where his innate faculties will have appeared in all their perfection. While this process is never-ending, the organization of mankind on the planet can achieve a final degree of perfection. It is to this goal – the unification of mankind – that history has been moving from the outset. Teilhard de Chardin wrote of this as 'the planet-ization of Mankind':

. . . Mankind, born on this planet and spread over its entire surface, coming gradually to form around its earthly matrix a single, major organic unity, enclosed upon itself; a single, hyper-complex, hyper-centred, hyper-conscious arch-molecule, co-extensive with the heavenly body on which it was born.[34]

This is the goal of evolution as far as humanity's ordered life is concerned. Up to this moment it has not been a possibility: 'Prehistory teaches us that in the beginning Man must have lived in small, autonomous groups; after which links were established, first between families and then between tribes. These associations became more elaborate as time went on.' Now the moment has occurred for a 'basic transformation, that is to say a change of major dimensions in the human state'.[35] Shoghi Effendi saw this change as requiring nothing less than 'the complete unification of the diverse elements that constitute human society':

This will indeed be the fitting climax of that process of integration which, starting with the family, the smallest unit in the scale of human organization, must, after having called successively into being the tribe, the city-state and the nation, continue to operate until it culminates in the unification of the whole world, *the final object and the crowning glory of human evolution on this planet*.[36]

Social evolution through history has been slow. According to Bahá'í teaching it has been closely allied with progressive, relative revelations of the Divine Spirit:

Just as the organic evolution of mankind has been slow and gradual, and involved successively the unification of the family, the tribe, the city-state, and the nation, so has the light vouchsafed by the Revelation of God, at various stages in the evolution of religion, and reflected in the successive Dispensations of the past, been slow and progressive. Indeed the measure of Divine Revelation, in every age, has been adapted to, and commensurate with, the degree of social progress achieved in that age by a constantly evolving humanity.[37]

Each revelation of the divinity established a limited degree of unity among men. Zoroaster joined the farmers of the Iranian plateau into a distinct geographical unity. Moses welded

34. T. de Chardin, *The Future of Man*, p. 120.
35. ibid. p. 41.
36. Shoghi Effendi, *The Promised Day Is Come*, p. 122 (italics mine).
37. ibid. p. 123.

together the tribes of Israel. Christ's message created a unity of faith within the Mediterranean and Northern European regions, and subsequently Muhammad made of the Arabs an entire nation from Baghdad to Granada. But 'Abdu'l-Bahá said: 'In cycles gone by, though harmony was established, yet, owing to the absence of means, the unity of all mankind could not have been achieved. Continents remained widely divided, nay even among peoples of one and the same continent association and interchange of thought were well-nigh impossible.'[38]

The situation at the beginning of the seventeenth century, Arnold Toynbee tells us, was that there were five 'living societies' in the world, each sufficient unto itself and largely uninfluenced by the others.[39] It was within the Western European Christian civilization that a movement was laid in that same century which would completely alter this: the ingenuity devoted to the natural sciences would eventually yield its greatest fruit in the creation of a world-revolutionizing technology. By the twentieth century this technology had diminished the separate geographical areas of the world until the planet had become one theatre – for travel, trade, the conflict of ideologies, and war.[40] Although within the twentieth century men have responded to the new situation and called for single world approaches to health, development, energy, currency – and many other matters embracing the common destiny of mankind – such attempts at international solidarity as the League of Nations and the United Nations have not received the kind of unified support necessary for their success. The unification of the planet is in fact coming about without the conscious, willing support of man himself.

Perhaps the most significant reason for the retardation of the process of unification has been the clinging to national sovereignty. 'Nation-building has come to an end', wrote Shoghi Effendi in 1936. 'The anarchy inherent in state

38. Shoghi Effendi, *The Promised Day Is Come*, p. 125.
39. See A. J. Toynbee, *A Study of History*, vol. I, p. 8.
40. For a précis of this process see Toynbee, *Civilization on Trial*.

sovereignty is moving towards a climax. A world, growing to maturity, must abandon this fetish, recognize the oneness and wholeness of human relationships, and establish once for all the machinery that can best incarnate this fundamental principle of its life.'[41] Yet the slowness of man's willingness to change assures a cataclysmic character to this stage in the evolutionary process. 'That the forces of a world catastrophe can alone precipitate such a new phase of human thought is, alas, becoming increasingly apparent.'[42]

Such a vital stage in human evolution, upon which human history for the next thousand years at least must depend, could not have arrived without preparation and guidance being provided by Providence. The Bahá'í concept of providential involvement in each crucial stage of man's evolution inevitably implies that the momentous stage of mankind's coming of age should synchronize with a new revelation of the divine will. If man doubted the necessity for divine intervention in the course of past evolution in man's destiny, he surely could not deny it at this stage, where humanity has become embroiled in conflict and beset by problems that appear to be Hydra-headed at each point he attempts a solution.

An Eschatology for the Modern Age

The twentieth century might, from the evidence of its conflicts and conflagrations manifesting deeds of brutality equal to anything perpetrated in the past, be called a dark age. Nevertheless, it has witnessed the establishment of cooperation and social schemes for the betterment of many; advances in medicine and living standards; and even the establishment of an international charter of human rights that men should ideally honour. It is evident that since the middle of the last century the human spirit has taken a gigantic leap forward. Intellectual and technological innovation has been prodigious. Yet for all that,

41. Shoghi Effendi, 'The Unfoldment of World Civilization', in *The World Order of Bahá'u'lláh*, p. 202.
42. 'The Goal of a New World Order', in *The World Order of Bahá'u'lláh*, p. 46.

in the last decades of the nineteenth century, artists and thinkers first began to experience despair. Their sense of hopelessness spread to ordinary people by the mid-twentieth century. The dreams of science turned into a nightmare; technology changed from being the saving force to being the destroying menace that created nuclear weaponry. Orthodox religions continued to regress – having lost the intelligentsia, they witnessed the disaffection of the masses. It needed no great profundity to diagnose a vacuum at the heart of the age. 'Mount into your railways,' Carlyle wrote in 1850, 'whirl from place to place, at the rate of fifty, or if you like of five hundred miles an hour: you cannot escape from that inexorable all-encircling ocean-moan of ennui.'

A materialist civilization will never satisfy the aspiration of man, let alone one riddled with such paradoxes as ours of the modern era. What if the advances in the realm of rational thought had been accompanied by an outpouring of the divine spirit, channelled through a new-born religion? Never before has mankind been in such need of revitalizing, of an *élan* that would restore to him his heavenly as well as his intellectual nature. In the first half of the last century, Europe was replete with the kind of idealism that was ready to grasp such a new spirit. Almost instinctively it threw up prophets and self-styled messiahs. Since then men of goodwill have called for brotherhood, the abandonment of prejudice, and the utilization of the new wealth and technology for all; laudable organizations have striven to promote peace and understanding. Yet the outlook grew bleaker because human behaviour stayed fundamentally the same.

At exactly the time the old religious orthodoxy began to crumble before the march of secularism and agnosticism, the Bahá'í Faith appeared in the world. The new faith was the pre-destined revelation of the divinity that synchronized with the creation of new movements in science and thought. The revelation of God thus accompanied profound changes in the development of the human spirit. Potentially, humanity was prepared for the age of maturity, the coming of age of mankind.

The role of the Bahá'í Faith was the presentation to the world of the divine teachings which would lead it into this new age. In time these teachings would inspire an unparalleled flowering of arts and sciences in a supreme, world civilization. The fundamental teaching of the new faith – the essential oneness of mankind – would bring about both the organizational and spiritual foundations for such a civilization. A world government was foreseen; a universal system of education; a world language, and a world system of measures. All these teachings were to provide the machinery of the new order, conceived by Bahá'u'lláh one hundred years ago. The spirit of love that alone would make it worthwhile was released through the Manifestation of God. The love and power of the Christ-Spirit is enough for a whole world – it alone can join the whole of mankind into one unity of faith. The practical channelling of this spirit was allowed for by the institutions conceived by the Manifestation for the ordering of mankind, and the exhortations and principles for the securing of a just distribution of wealth, and protection of the weak.

In fact, the teachings for the new age covered every aspect of human activity. Never before had religion so embraced the entirety of human experience, speaking no longer in parables and occult symbols. Rational answers and rational proofs were advanced; science and religion were joined in the service of mankind. The Bahá'í teachings represented a harmonizing of every principle within the human constitution, an answer to every aspiration. They stand today, not as a forbidding monolith exacting obedience and conformity, but a growing organism, nurturing the total cohesiveness and individual uniqueness in mankind as we see it in the natural creation.

Man's rejection of this absolutely fundamental power in the progress toward the goal of history represented a tragic hiatus in his immediate development. It meant that the accomplishment of this vital stage in mankind's evolution – likened by Shoghi Effendi to the crucial years attending the age of consent in the individual – would now necessarily be traumatic and turbulent. When Bahá'u'lláh wrote to the world's leaders apprising them of his message for mankind, and when 'Abdu'l-Bahá brought it to the western world, humanity was given the chance to embrace the new revelation. The responsibility for rejecting or ignoring it rests heavily upon the world's leaders then and now, but mankind has long since moved beyond its shelter.

The eschatology of the Semitic religions appears arbitrary and mythical to the modern mind. The great physical upheavals in the earth and heavens, if literally to occur, would leave no planet earth. But beneath the abstruse language of these prophecies lies a sure presentation of the times through which we are living. We only deride the advocates of this eschatology because they have given it a literal interpretation. According to the Bahá'í view, the prophets were given a foreknowledge of events in visions they themselves barely understood.

Mankind has passed into the era of war and catastrophe foretold by Christ. Everywhere hopes lie shattered. The time of the end has come; we are witnessing a judgement prolonged since the outbreak of the Great War in 1914; 'and when the appointed hour is come', promised Bahá'u'lláh, 'there shall appear that which shall cause the limbs of mankind to quake'. 'This judgement of God', explains Shoghi Effendi, 'is both a retributory calamity and an act of holy and supreme discipline. It is at once a visitation from God and a cleansing process for all mankind. Its fires punish the perversity of the human race, and weld its component parts into one organic, indivisible, world-embracing community.'[43] Providence rules the 'Last Day' through a decaying human society, and the natural forces of earthquakes and other world-shaking phenomena. The purpose is not blind destruction but the reorganizing of the human race. 'Adversity, prolonged, world-wide, afflictive, allied to chaos and universal destruction, must needs convulse the nations, stir the conscience of the world, disillusion the masses, precipitate a radical change in the very conception of society . . .'[44] Such a plan is purposive, having as its aim, as

43. Shoghi Effendi, *The Promised Day Is Come*, p.2.
44. ibid. p. 127.

Shoghi Effendi reiterates, the coalescing of 'the disjointed bleeding limbs of mankind into one body, single, organically united, and indivisible'.[45]

The Bahá'í understanding of the end of the world is thus wholly in keeping with its evolutionary view of history. Mankind has wandered far from the path – the purpose of the calamity of the end times is to awaken it and bring it back. But out of the ordeal a new humanity will emerge, not re-made by some divine *fiat*, but chastened by experience and ready to cooperate with God in building the long-promised kingdom of heaven on the earth. Such an eschatology answers much more clearly to human experience as we know it than the various fantasies of fundamentalist religious groups.

The Golden Age

Again we have to acknowledge that this view of the modern age extended by the Bahá'í teachings (and the view of the distant future which they also offer) cannot be accounted empirical in its derivation; it must be termed prophetic, inasmuch as it claims to foretell the future. No doubt this is not qualified to be called a historical approach. If it is a 'philosophy of history' it also errs, as such schemes are wont to, in 'speculation', for which it can offer no necessary proof. The Bahá'í Faith stands guilty of such 'indiscretions', as Bahá'u'lláh was 'indiscreet' in his summons of mankind to world unity one hundred years ago.

Bahá'u'lláh's prophetic vision embraced not just this age but the entire course of history. He informed the world's rulers that since they had ignored the Most Great Peace extended to them as the Cause of God, they could still establish the 'lesser peace' themselves. This was a politically achieved peace which 'Abdu'l-Bahá promised later would be initiated by the close of the twentieth century. When this was established, mankind could begin to bring about those things Bahá'u'lláh had spoken of, and the unity of mankind would proceed, at first prag-

45. ibid.

matically, until mankind caught up the spirit of the millennium, and recognized the Faith of Bahá'u'lláh. Then the 'Most Great Peace', foretold by Bahá'u'lláh, would be established. This would coincide with the golden age of human history. Shoghi Effendi described the process:

. . . this consummation will, by its very nature, be a gradual process, and must, as Bahá'u'lláh has Himself anticipated, lead at first to the establishment of that Lesser Peace which the nations of the earth, as yet unconscious of His Revelation and yet unwittingly enforcing the general principles which He has enunciated, will themselves establish. This . . . will bring in its wake the spiritualization of the masses, consequent to the recognition of the character . . . and the acknowledgement of the claims, of the Faith of Bahá'u'lláh . . .[46]

It should be recognized that the 'Most Great Peace' constituting the new world order of Bahá'u'lláh, dimly as we can imagine what such a glorious order will be like, will be fundamentally spiritual in character. For all its perfection of material organization, its glory will consist in its quality of spiritual men – a 'new race of men', who will reflect the perfections of God. The aim in building this new world is far indeed from the establishment of the kind of godless Utopia written into the creeds of modern atheist philosophies. Yet these too have suggested to men a dull image of what their perfection might be. We might return to the words of Teilhard de Chardin to answer the misgivings of those who hold man so incorrigibly a sinner as to be incapable of such advance:

Our modern world was created in less than 10,000 years, and in the past 200 years it has changed more than in all the preceding millennia. Have we ever thought of what our planet may be like, psychologically, in a million years' time? It is finally the Utopians, not the 'realists', who make scientific sense. They at least, though their flights of fancy may cause us to smile, have a feeling for the true dimensions of the phenomenon of Man.[47]

To Shoghi Effendi, whose view of man was not in the least utopian, we must turn for a final vision of what mankind, according to the Bahá'í philosophy of history, has within reach:

46. Shoghi Effendi, *The Promised Day Is Come*, p. 128.
47. T. de Chardin, op. cit., p. 74.

National rivalries, hatreds, and intrigues will cease, and racial animosity and prejudice will be replaced by racial amity, understanding and cooperation. The causes of religious strife will be permanently removed, economic barriers and restrictions will be completely abolished, and the inordinate distinction between classes will be obliterated. Destitution on the one hand, and gross accumulation of ownership on the other, will disappear. The enormous energy dissipated and wasted on war, whether economic or political, will be consecrated to such ends as will extend the range of human inventions and technical development, to the increase of the productivity of mankind, to the extermination of disease, to the extension of scientific research, to the raising of the standard of physical health, to the sharpening and refinement of the human brain, to the exploitation of the unused and unsuspected resources of the planet, to the prolongation of human life, and to the furtherance of any other agency that can stimulate the intellectual, the moral, and spiritual life of the entire human race.

A world federal system, ruling the whole earth and exercising unchallengeable authority over its unimaginably vast resources, blending and embodying the ideals of both the East and the West, liberated from the curse of war and its miseries, and bent on the exploitation of all the available sources of energy on the surface of the planet, a system in which Force is made the servant of Justice, whose life is sustained by its universal recognition of one God and by its allegiance to one common Revelation – such is the goal towards which humanity, impelled by the unifying forces of life, is moving. [48]

48. Shoghi Effendi, 'The Unfoldment of World Civilization', in *The World Order of Bahá'u'lláh*, p. 204.

The Bahá'í Faith and Political Theory

> The teachings of Bahá'u'lláh are such that all the communities of the world, whether religious, political or ethical, ancient or modern, find in them the expression of their highest wish.
>
> *'Abdu'l-Bahá*[1]

WE MUST SURELY consider as a major calamity the failure of the world community to originate a universally accepted political order. Since the last century the theory and practice of government have throughout the world been revolutionized. Western civilization has led the world community in overthrowing feudalistic government and its associate absolutist centring of power. The French Revolution at the end of the eighteenth century and the American Revolution of the same period introduced concepts of freedom and equality before the law which have become embodied in twentieth-century formulations of human rights. In addition, more extreme revolutionary theories have gone beyond the belief that individual legal rights are sacrosanct, and have argued that the common people have been throughout history disenfranchised by property qualifications, and that private property itself is the last bulwark against human freedom.

The bourgeois revolutionaries in France and America desired to create a political state in which the freedoms and possessions of their class were guaranteed; they construed the

1. To the Executive Committee of the Central Organization for a Durable Peace, The Hague, 1919.

state as a contract entered into by rational individuals, designed
to safeguard their interests. To what extent the more extreme
Jacobins espoused communistic, collectivist ideas is still not
agreed upon today; but undoubtedly the French Revolution
also fathered the kind of egalitarian socialistic views that were
to be developed later in the left-wing movements of the
nineteenth and twentieth centuries.

In the political revolutions in Europe of 1830, 1848 and 1870
ideas of democracy, socialism and nationalism all played a part.
As the century wore on, however, conservative ideas also
began to achieve specific formulation, although the royalist
legitimism of the *ancien régime* was being replaced by right-
wing ideas that placed less stress on monarchical dynasties, and
more on the unity and mystique of the nation. The process of
industrialization in Western Europe, and its creation of a large
bourgeoisie and proletariat, changed the order of society
radically. Aristocracies were on the retreat as the bourgeoisie
challenged for a political power that was commensurate with
its newly acquired economic power.

The impact of Western ideas and technology spread from the
early years of the nineteenth century. Napoleon had invaded
Egypt and France introduced revolutionary ideas and
centralized organization into North Africa. Within thirty years
the Egyptian Khedive, Muḥammad 'Alí, was able to defeat an
Ottoman Turkish fleet as a result of organizing his forces on
European lines. The British strengthened their hold on India,
and in the 1830s began to implement English educational
methods among the Indian middle classes.

It is true that the Islamic world remained in a torpor; Turkey
was 'the sick man of Europe', and the Qájár dynasty in Persia
was incapable of maintaining its borders without the support of
Russia and Britain, and possessed no army to speak of. British
power brutally revealed the weakness of China in the Opium
War of the 1840s, and Japan was still in quarantine.

Yet with the growth of Europe's industrial economic might,
it was only a matter of time before its power spread throughout
the globe, partitioning it off into areas of European nations'

influence. In Africa, in the last quarter of the century, this European power expressed itself in a naked imperialism. National rivalries among the Europeans ensured that the continent was rapidly prospected and divided up, often, as in the case of the incident at Fashoda in East Africa in 1898, bringing European powers to the verge of war.

The humiliation of ancient cultures like those of China and Japan by Western power led to different responses: the Chinese endeavoured to shut the West out; Japan rapidly adopted Western technology and organization to such good measure that it was able to inflict a military defeat on a European power – Russia – in 1905–6.

The impact of the new industrial technology on the relations between states was portentous: Bismarck united the German states by clever diplomacy, but he had the increasingly formidable military might of Prussia behind him. In 1870 the Prussians defeated the antiquated French cavalry by superior mechanization, including the use of railways to transport troops. The growing material power at the disposal of European governments was accompanied by increasing antagonism, jealousy and mutual fear. Nationalism, which in the first part of the nineteenth century was encouraged by idealistic, cosmopolitan figures like Mazzini and Garibaldi, degenerated in the latter half into a struggle for supremacy that was to lead to the world conflicts of states between 1914–18 and 1939–45.

The Establishment of Secular Politics

All through this period the influence of secular politics grew. Hitherto concentrated in the hands of a very small few, and usually associated with land and the hereditary principle, power became more diffuse and political theory altered to meet the new socio-economic realities. In the old order, or *ancien régime*, kings derived their powers directly from God, and in most states religion and monarch came to some kind of agreement. Monarchs in Catholic countries maintained the

Catholic faith, and Protestant monarchs the Protestant faith. If an aspiring monarch had a different religion to the religion of the state over which he wished to rule, invariably he would be expected to change it, as in the case of Henri of Navarre, who gave up his Protestantism to become Henri IV of France. In the Europe of the *ancien régime* politics and religion were closely entwined, and His Majesty's subjects were expected, at the whim of their monarch, to fight for God, King and Fatherland. So close was the identity between religion and monarch in nineteenth-century Russia that when the Tsars were finally removed by a popular revolution the clergy and ecclesiastical organization were thrown out too. The Robespierrists in France replaced the Catholicism of the old monarchist state with a new religion of the revolution. And in the Turkish republic that replaced the Sultanate in the 1920s Muslim clerics lost all their powers and state law was secularized.

One of the reasons for the decline of religion in the modern world and the secularization of every part of life rests with the antiquated character of so many of the religious institutions of the world, and their association with a dying social order. The left-wing political forces realized that their battle for power must involve attacking the conservative force of religion, and Marxist atheism has become a militant foe of religion wherever it encounters it.

Right-wing nationalism has replaced God with the deified state. National Socialism had no qualms about reviving pagan rites and symbols in an ostensibly Christian Germany. In Spain, however, the Catholic Church supported Franco's Phalangist regime in return for state approval of religion. In Iran the Pahlavi Shahs gave some indulgence to Islam, but set about creating a myth of Aryan glory mixing nationalistic and monarchist doctrines which the Shí'i mullas branded atheistic and pagan.

The growth of secularism accompanied the spread of scientific and rationalist theories, and political ideas invoked their aid. Marxism's claim to be scientifically founded was echoed in the racialist theories of the extreme right, which claimed racial superiority to be scientific fact. Even liberal democracy was nourished with rational and scientific frames of thought, particularly as so many nineteenth-century liberals believed in the advance of science as a matter of faith, and in the idea of progress toward a perfectly organized society.

The secularization of politics has led to the atomization of world society that we see today: political theories of different varieties, at first established upon ideas of progress, have multiplied, and political parties which bear their stamp have also mushroomed. Personal interests have also played their part until every new political faction seems only to further the disarray of the modern world. Truly, no two men can be found who can be called inwardly and outwardly united: the creation of a politically diverse world has, if we regard the world of today, undoubtedly failed to advance the human race on the path of cooperation and peace. At the same time the ever-increasing interest in political pursuits, among greater and greater sections of humanity, has been accompanied by an inversely proportional departure from the practice of religion. Ancient religious antagonisms have once again surfaced as well, linked with more recent nationalistic and ideological rivalries.

As for the creative spirit of religion, in the words of Shoghi Effendi:

This vital force is dying out, this mighty agency has been scorned, this radiant light is obscured, this impregnable stronghold abandoned, this beauteous robe discarded. God himself has indeed been dethroned from the hearts of men, and an idolatrous world passionately and clamorously hails and worships the false gods which its own idle fancies have fatuously created, and its misguided hands so impiously exalted. The chief idols in the desecrated temple of mankind are none other than the triple gods of Nationalism, Racialism and Communism, at whose altars governments and peoples, whether democratic or totalitarian, at peace or at war, of the East or of the West, Christian or Islamic, are, in various forms and in different degrees now worshipping.[2]

2. *The Promised Day Is Come*, p. 117.

Liberal Democracy in the West

Definitions of democracy are notoriously difficult to arrive at: both Western capitalist and Eastern communist systems claim to be the true custodians of the democratic principle. Dictatorships of the worst kind have been built upon democratic processes – the Nazis were able to seize power in Germany as a result of successes at the polls.

At the beginning, democracy was always a limited process: even in ancient Athens it never spread beyond the educated classes. Eighteenth-century advocates of democratic freedoms such as the American founding fathers had views as to how far the democratic franchise could be spread. The bourgeois revolutionaries of the Third Estate who effected the French Revolution of 1789 had no intention of turning power over to the lower classes. Liberal democracy as we know it in the West developed out of the revolt of the middle classes against aristocratic oligarchy and monarchic absolutism; its founding fathers were professional men – businessmen and lawyers – men of the world, who were above all practical, and whose interest in freedom centred on their personal aspirations and confidence of taking over from a corrupt and inefficient aristocracy.

Initially, democracy was tried out under commensurately protected conditions: in England the 1832 Reform Bill admitted many of the manufacturing middle classes to the franchise, but even so, barely one Briton in five had the vote after its passing. The same was true of France, although the franchise was widened there in periods of revolutionary activity. Liberal democracy worked well in the nineteenth century because it suited the requirements of societies in which the middle classes more and more became the real originators of economic change, and thus the shapers of social attitudes.

By the time it was deemed safe to admit the whole population into the franchise the middle classes had succeeded in establishing effective control over the institutions and machinery of government. The result of this was in fact a spreading of middle-class values to other sections of society, and social-democratic and labour governments were able to take power in most of the European countries in the early twentieth century without bringing about bloody revolution.

The watchword of this system of politics is freedom, and having its basis in the economic individualism of the capitalist system of economics, it has succeeded in maintaining certain basic freedoms: freedom of speech and of the press, freedom of association and freedom of religious belief. These freedoms are important ones in any society, and when lost, represent a serious reversal.

Liberal democracy is primarily a Western phenomenon, and is not always assimilable to societies marked by strong age-old ties of tribal or family unity and loyalty with different concepts of social responsibility. In fact, as Marx rightly pointed out well over a century ago, it is the province of capitalism, the economic order upon which liberal democracy has been built, to break down all such ties, leaving in its wake the destruction of all bonds but that of wage-earner and entrepreneur. A system of social order like the capitalist one can also afford to be tolerant of every religious principle, for being essentially a materialistic order, it has little interest in religion. It is true that sections of the middle classes have, in capitalist societies, identified the virtues of a *laissez-faire* business economy with Christianity, but this at the expense of its founder's cardinal principle that you cannot serve God and Mammon. Today, the Western democracies might be said to be as devoid of spiritual direction as the socialist system of Eastern Europe.

This, according to Shoghi Effendi, is certainly the Bahá'í view of the apparent ideological split between East and West. It is indeed vital, in understanding the alternative order proffered in the Bahá'í teachings, to recognize the fundamental divergence of the Bahá'í order from either of the above social and economic systems, or indeed any other extant in the world at present. For the Bahá'í order, while embodying the beneficial aspects of monarchy, aristocracy and democracy, excludes their harmful aspects, and cannot be identified with any of them. Critics of the Bahá'í Administrative Order have maintained that it is specifically pro-monarchist and anti-socialist and anti-communist; we shall compare the philosophy of the left with that of the Bahá'í Faith presently: it is for the moment important to stress that any criticism that seeks to identify the Bahá'í view with that either of the right or the left, the democratic or totalitarian, is essentially misdirected. Indeed, the Bahá'í system, properly speaking, is not 'anti' any system of government, as is evidenced by the refusal of Bahá'í institutions as well as individuals, as an article of faith, to become involved in politics. And further: no one can be compelled to be a Bahá'í, just as the right of an individual to withdraw from the Bahá'í community is upheld and respected. Moreover, the rights of minorities are especially proclaimed and nurtured within the Bahá'í system – in stark contrast to the attitudes and practices of most movements working for an ideal world at present, whose attempts to coerce other human beings to accept and abide by their ideas account in large measure for the terrible wars, persecutions and pogroms which have been witnessed in the twentieth century.

This does not mean, however, that in the Bahá'í commonwealth all citizens will not be expected to obey the same law, which will be that prescribed in the teachings of the Bahá'í Faith. This would be merely the application of a general principle that the only fair way of running a state is for the majority will to be obeyed, albeit with the proviso mentioned above: that special attention is paid to the rights and needs of minorities. Ends cannot be divorced from means: at present a minority wherever they dwell, Bahá'í communities are obedient to the laws of the lands in which they function.

Though we have parted somewhat from our discussion of the system of liberal democracy in the West, it has been necessary in order to establish the basis of a Bahá'í critique. Our intention, when comparing this system with that prescribed by the Bahá'í teachings, and also in comparing the other systems in this section, is not to attack specific governments or states – since this would be opposed to the Bahá'í principle of political neutrality and civil obedience – but to make a comparison between theories of government and social development. There will be elements in some of these systems which Bahá'ís could accept, but overall, by the very nature of the challenge implicit in the Bahá'í revelation, there must also be fundamental divergence.

Liberal democracy has been constructive in its nurturing of certain liberties – such as liberty of conscience and freedom of expression – and to these principles in general Bahá'ís would also assent. The practice of democracy in the West is based upon a system of propagandizing and electioneering which is unacceptable to the Bahá'í view of election and consultation, where the practice of canvassing and nomination is expressly forbidden. In the Bahá'í system elected representatives are not responsible to party caucuses (which would in any case be non-existent in the Bahá'í order) or even to the electorate, but only to their own consciences.

The most important divergence between the two systems, however, is one of aim: the Bahá'í order is founded upon spiritual principles, and indeed is organically dependent upon them for its healthy functioning. Shoghi Effendi reiterated the fact that without the Bahá'í spirit, the Administrative Order prescribed by Bahá'u'lláh would be a lifeless body, however perfect its structure. The liberal democratic system, in contrast, could be described as a body without a spirit: it purposely leaves the spiritual aspects of life to be expressed – or not expressed – by the individual conscience. Indeed, its proponents sometimes point this out as a mark of its success: the liberal democratic system is meant to provide just as much government as is necessary, leaving the enrichment of social life to the qualities of its members. But the decline of religion and the advance of materialistic values has all but negated this aspect of Western society, so that what we are left with is a society which 'Abdu'l-Bahá called 'morally uncivilized'. The threat hanging over such a society is surely that presaged by Bahá'u'lláh, when he warned of the 'flame' that would 'devour the cities' when civilization was carried to excess.

The Challenge of the Left

Marxism has an importance much larger than a mere political creed – it has been called a 'religious irreligion', and is accounted as an atheistic religion by some scholars of belief.

The appeal of Marxism is not hard to understand: it offers hope to the masses of mankind that their material conditions can be changed, and they themselves hold power over their own destiny. Marxism teaches the inevitability of the victory of the working classes or proletariat over the powerful political and economic forces wielded by other classes in the world today. It teaches that these classes – above all, the middle classes, or bourgeoisie, that stand associated with the capitalist system of economics – will be conquered by the combined power of the proletariat. Although Marx and Engels based this teaching on 'laws of history' which they claimed to have discovered, the belief in the eventual triumph of the proletariat is held by many modern followers with an almost religious firmness. Thus, although the main premise of Marxism is that it is scientifically founded, its beliefs are often held with something like religious assurance.

However, Marx insisted on a materialistic interpretation of the world – that is to say, he denied the traditional religious doctrines of the existence of God and the immortality of the soul. He went against the idealist philosophers who taught that spirit or idea was the ultimate reality, and insisted instead that the material was the only reality. Accordingly, his interpretation of history rests on the idea that man is an economic animal, and that history, in the words of the Communist Manifesto, 'is the history of class struggles'.

Marx learnt from the German philosopher Hegel that life was fundamentally a process of challenge, that for every process of development in the world there was a law of change which Hegel called the dialectic. In dialectic theory an idea is challenged by its complete opposite, and the result is that a synthesis, or combining of the best elements of both is achieved. But where Hegel talked of ideas in the abstract, Marx insisted that his theory was only applicable to social and economic forces. He divided the history of societies into a primitive communist stage, where all property was held in common; a feudal stage, where society was divided into peasants and noblemen; and a bourgeois stage, in which industrial society of the modern type was established, and economic power was concentrated in the hands of the entrepreneur or capitalist. This stage saw the confrontation of two opposing classes, the bourgeoisie and the proletariat – and the clash between them would result in the victory of the proletariat, but in a changed form. A socialist society would emerge that eventually would become a communist one. The communist society would be a perfect classless society and the final development of society. The clash of different forms of social organization occurred at critical moments in history, and in Marxism such moments were called revolutionary – the purpose of the Marxist today is to fight for the revolution in which the proletariat will finally triumph.

Marxism is therefore founded on the teaching that the oppressed peoples of the world will rise and seize power for themselves. It is an economic and a political philosophy, but it has messianic and millennial overtones – that is to say: it supports the hope of a perfect society within the reach of man. Today is the time when such a society can be established. Messianism involves the expectancy of a messiah – Marxism has its messiahs in Marx and Engels and revolutionary leaders like Lenin, Stalin and Mao-tse-Tung.

Comparison with the Bahá'í teachings reveals important similarities, fundamental disagreements, and areas where the Bahá'í teachings perfect the aspirations of the Marxists.

First of all, both Marxism and the Bahá'í Faith place great importance on history, and upon the change in society that has taken place in the last hundred and fifty years. Both stress the unifying aspect of the modern age, where economic and intellectual forces have combined with technology to create an interdependent world.

Both interpret the past in terms of the evolution of limited stages of development until a universal one is reached. The universal stage in Marxism is the world communist, classless society; in the Bahá'í Faith it is the world commonwealth uniting all races and classes in one universal religion. Both creeds expect the universal stage to be a perfect one as far as social organization is concerned; both believe that this stage will see the end of oppression and injustice, and the emancipation of the masses of mankind.

Before we compare their social teaching however, it must be said that in several vital matters there is profound disagreement. The Bahá'í Faith affirms the existence of God, and insists that man can only achieve true progress by turning to God and his Manifestations. Marxism, as we saw, is atheistic, and says that man can achieve his social salvation alone: it claims that although Christianity was a revolutionary force to begin with, it became reactionary later on, and that religion more often than not makes people accept the present order in the hope of better things in the next world. Marx called this kind of religion an opiate. At closer inspection, we can see that the Bahá'í Faith also discriminates between religion when it is fresh and young and able to change man and society, as opposed to when it becomes dogmatic and old, and maintains backward traditions and antagonism. But at heart, Marxism and the Bahá'í Faith differ over their view of man and society: Marxism sees man as an economic animal only, whereas the Bahá'í teaching is that man is essentially a spiritual being. Although Marxism aims at a peaceful and cooperative society, it is prepared to adopt violent means to achieve this. The Bahá'í teachings aim at unifying different forces rather than having one triumph at the expense of another.

Indeed, the social teachings of the two creeds differ on this very point. Marxism sees human society as founded upon antagonism and struggle; the Bahá'í Faith aims at harmonizing conflicting interests through the power of religion. The Bahá'í Faith states that fundamentally man can overcome his difficulties only by becoming spiritual and caring towards his fellow man. Marxism lacks this dimension. Bahá'í teachings therefore do not permit the destruction of any class, and they do not claim that a classless society can be achieved, for 'difference of capacity in human individuals is fundamental. It is impossible for all to be alike, all to be equal, all to be wise.'

The Bahá'í social teachings are far closer to those of the French socialist, Saint-Simon, who said that different classes would remain, and that captains and men of knowledge in particular must lead society, but who hoped for a new religion to cement the different classes together and make them sacrifice for one another: However, on the matter of class the Bahá'í teachings do not go into detail. We might expect the present social divisions in the world to be softened and transmuted in a future Bahá'í order.

On one other important matter as well, the Bahá'í teachings are not specific and detailed: that of the solution to economic problems. A 'spiritual solution' is prescribed, but this solution is left for the future to implement. There is no subject upon which ideologies have proved less firm than the question of economics. Communist governments have introduced limited measures of free enterprise into state-controlled economies, and capitalist societies have invoked varying degrees of public ownership. Other interests have demanded the break-up of centralized control over economic life, and have called for social ownership on a smaller community scale. From 'Abdu'l-Bahá's talks in the West it might be concluded that some favour, in a future Bahá'í system, might well be shown to the last principle. However, no firm economic judgements are made in the Bahá'í teachings other than that extremes of wealth and poverty must be abolished. Philanthropy is encouraged, but the community will also exact taxes on the better-off to ensure the well-being of all its members. Individual enterprise is certainly not prohibited, but given the orientation of the whole of Bahá'í affairs towards the community it seems unlikely that private enterprise as we know it today – with its concentration of wealth in the hands of a small few – will be reproduced in the Bahá'í commonwealth. The prescription of profit-sharing – which *is* a firm teaching of economic application found in the Bahá'í Faith – further reinforces this view. Indeed, the nature of Bahá'í decision-making, which is essentially corporate, and unattached to economic interests, suggests that the excesses of capitalism will be removed, albeit without the extreme economic measures demanded by the 'hard' left philosophies. Private property will continue and enterprise will too. Wealth is of great importance to the whole of society, and yet its creation is, in the last resort, dependent on the leadership and expertise of individuals.

In conclusion: the aim of establishing brotherhood amongst men and eradicating injustice and poverty is laudable, and thus far Marxist and Bahá'í theories concur; however, as with the liberal democratic and capitalist system, the materialist axioms at the heart of Marxism are unacceptable to Bahá'ís. It is the godlessness of Communist theory which called upon it Shoghi Effendi's severest castigation. He identified it as one of the three 'false gods' of modern society.

Right-wing Nationalism

Totalitarian movements of both the left and the right have certain common features; the philosophical background in Germany in the 1840s which contributed to the growth of Marxism also helped form the cult of power and messianic leadership that eventually yielded the National Socialist German Workers' Party of Adolf Hitler.

Nationalism as practised today was an important by-product of the Napoleonic period in European history, and at first the attempts to unite the nations of Italy and Germany were led by liberals and idealists. That both countries were eventually united by force of arms showed that in the real world national interest could only be pursued at the expense of other powers. Bismarck was the first to call treaties pieces of paper, and his predominating concern for the interests of his own nation before all else became a feature of late nineteenth-century and early twentieth-century politics. Hitler was to carry the implication even further in breaking the Treaty of

Versailles, marching into the Rhineland, and finally invading Czechoslovakia and Poland.

Nationalism became perhaps the strongest motivating factor in international politics, and theorists of the right in France, Germany and even Great Britain exalted the nation as the highest legitimate authority. Attached to this exaltation of the nation went an insidious racialism that exalted Teuton above Slav, German above Frenchman and Aryan above Jew. This evil force would lead to the extermination of millions of Jews, Slavs, Romany people and others in the concentration camps of Hitler. Indeed, nationalism has become a pervasive aspect of the modern world, not limited to right-wing ideologies alone. It has become a cruel and terrible false god indeed, and bears the responsibility for countless deaths and destruction. The Bahá'í order must be by its very nature implacably opposed to nationalism and its accompanying narrowness of vision.

The universalism of Bahá'í teaching ensured the closing down of Bahá'í activities in Germany by the Nazis – there could hardly be a creed more diametrically different to Nazism with its racial theory and rampant nationalism than the Bahá'í one of internationalism, racial intermixture and the brotherhood of nations. A 'sane and intelligent patriotism' is not precluded to Bahá'ís, but their essential belief is in the wider loyalty to mankind as a whole.

The Flaw of Pluralism

Although the ordinary man today might well yearn for a truce between the warring political ideologies of our world, the hope that men may come to tolerate one another's political systems grows daily more forlorn. In the late forties Arnold Toynbee observed that mankind had only two options: either it must live permanently divided into two camps, preferably with the minimum of intercourse or with the firm agreement of non-interference one with the other, or one of the two superpowers had to eliminate or absorb the other and establish a unitary order in the world. Since that time the two superpowers have several times come close to clashing, and have fought by proxy numerous wars with each other. The world is deeply divided politically, yet it is growing ever more integrated economically. It is in fact impossible for the human community of nations to ignore the centrifugal pull towards a unified system of economics, as well as all the subsidiary systems of world cooperation that grow daily more essential for the ordered life of man on his planet.

Pluralism cannot work because the different political systems cannot in practice keep apart by marking off respective spheres of influence. Pragmatism might indicate that given time they might 'rub together' and find common ground in give and take. Unfortunately we have not the time for this – the world is being bled by the arms race, and its economic order, on the verge of collapse as a result of the absurd expenditure a majority of states devote to arms, can scarcely survive into the next decade.

The present order of separate blocks of nations, divided by political ideology, but endeavouring to trade together, cannot long last. The most likely course of events is therefore that a third world war will ensue. If a section of humanity survives this, it will have to begin anew.

The Bahá'í Challenge for the Future

By the end of the twentieth century mankind must therefore witness the establishment of a new political order in the world. It will no doubt be governed by exigency, but its first priority must be to outlaw war for ever, and to rebuild the planet in the name of the entire human race.

The pressing problem will be to feed the human race, and there will have to be a return to agriculture as the primary human occupation. Many, perhaps all, of the industrialized centres of the world may have been destroyed. However, man will succeed in building a new material civilization – he usually has in the past – founded on a basic political unity, this in time devoted to mankind as a whole rather than the interests of powerful nations alone. In such a system it is unlikely that religion will, at first, play a part. Nevertheless, men will surely discover a spiritual vacuum at the core of their lives: they may even consider inventing a religion of their own, for it is not to be expected that they will return to the discredited faiths of the past.

Where will men find the following principles and beliefs with which to enrich their society and individual lives?

1. Unity of conscience – the sure basis of securing a lasting peace.
2. Cooperation – including the voluntary sharing of wealth.
3. Profit-sharing – ensuring that workers receive a share of profits and an interest in their work.
4. Graduated income tax – so that the community will be able to support the infirm, orphans and the weak out of a common fund.
5. Universal participation of the people in affairs of the community.
6. The outlawing of excessive wealth.
7. The abolition of poverty – so that *all* live in the 'utmost comfort'.
8. The encouragement of agriculture and the concentrating of resources on agricultural communities.

Such principles are found in the Bahá'í Faith. They imply a radical change of emphasis from the values of today, particularly of the industrial West. They appeal to the world's masses, who overwhelmingly dwell in villages and small towns. They disown the mammonism of contemporary capitalism, with its detachment from the roots of our existence, the basis of production itself: the earth. They answer to a need increasingly recognized among those alienated by the greed and selfishness of modern civilization: that of cooperation rather than competition, of community rather than corporations.

The Bahá'í teachings recognize the need for an entrepreneurial class, but subordinate the power of that class to the control of the community as a whole. They seek to soften greatly the class divisions of our age, and by stressing the value of useful education and crafts encourage all to play their part. The position of teachers is upraised; artisans, artists, scientists, doctors and nurses are venerated. Above all, the spiritual impulse found in the teachings of the Bahá'í Faith means that social awareness will grow: individuals, families, tribes will no longer be isolated units. Society will be organically structured – the different sections will contribute their part to the whole, and the social cement will be faith in God and respect for man.

Men of the future may well favour such a set of principles, and they will be even more ready to do so if they can see them already operating in practice. The challenge of the Bahá'í order will be seen to work if it can demonstrate in the future that it has raised human beings to a higher level of humanity. Such a religion, integrally associated with the everyday life of man, and not merely with his 'spiritual life', would illuminate the area designated for practical politics at present. For it will constitute a new kind of politics no longer based on greed and suspicion; it presupposes that man in society will act according to the principles of the Faith, not according to some 'practical' standard associated with the 'worldly' values of today's marketplace. At its heart is the principle that every human being is created by God, 'that no man should exalt himself over another'.

The future of the Bahá'í Faith therefore lies in the hands of all mankind. It is extremely doubtful whether its critics, or even its supporters, now fully appreciate its radical potential or the change in social and cultural attitudes its implementation implies. It is the fulfilment of Christ's promise that the meek shall inherit the earth, and embodies the spirit we find in the Sermon on the Mount, that inspiration for generations of reformers who have prayed, in the words of the Gospel, to see the corrupt and mighty thrown down from their seats, and the weak and humble gain access to their rightful heritage on this earth. The Almighty, Bahá'u'lláh informs us, wishes to see the human race as one soul, eating with the same mouth and walking with the same feet. How will injustice retain its sway if this is His plan for His sons and daughters on earth?

For the teachings of Bahá'u'lláh are far more essential than any philosophy or scheme for social transformation at present claiming adherents. They involve both a change in the heart of every man, and a change in the organization of society. They are, however, constructive, and in no sense destructive of what has proven of benefit and worth to the human race thus far in its development – to that degree they may be said to endorse the best that tradition can offer. For example: Bahá'í teaching venerates the family as the core of society; it endorses high standards of personal conduct and places the onus on the individual for following the strictest standards of rectitude. Revolutionaries of our time have too often dismissed ethics altogether, and have claimed the ends justified the means. The Bahá'í Faith is not a political programme for change – it is far more profound than that. It says that man can change himself, that he can climb to a higher stage in his evolution, leaving beside his former self, and entering a new stage in which his spiritual faculties, dormant till now, are more fully developed. This is the meaning of Christ's promise that the 'Kingdom of Heaven' would come, and be established on this earth. The process will be a painful one, and will not be ushered in overnight, but the claim of the Bahá'í Faith – the most idealistic but at the same time the most practical and exciting – is that it can be done.

But in practice what will this mean? Sceptics would be justified in refusing to submit immediately to the optimism of the faithful. Why won't the Bahá'í order, consisting of human beings as it must, become as tyrannical as past absolute polities – especially those with theocratic pretensions? The answer rests on the respect for the conscience of the individual and safeguarding of the rights of minorities already discussed, added to the success of the Bahá'í order in its claim of answering to the Spirit of the Age: for the Bahá'í Faith represents the unifying of the ancient promise of the Holy Spirit and the modern principle of evolution. Implicit in its seemingly impossible standards of individual and social behaviour is the sense that man is on the threshold of a new stage in his evolution; the past is insufficient to predicate the changes of the future. In a very real sense Bahá'u'lláh has abrogated the tragic past. His Revelation is alone sufficient for the future. Will it prove creative, will man take it up? – that remains to be seen.

The Modern Apocalypse

'MEN ARE AS THE TIME IS' says a character in *King Lear*; a maxim attributed to 'Alí Ibn Abú Ṭálib runs: 'Men are more like the time in which they live, than they are like their fathers.' Even prophets and seers outrun their own age in the visions they see, only to be bemused, true sons of their time, by the prophecies to which their timeless faculty has given birth. Nostradamus foresees explosions emanating from the sky, and a man named 'Hister' troubling an age too unlike his own world of plague, famine and the heretic's and sorcerer's fire to worry any more than his astrologer's fancy. So even more are the multitudes of the once-living inclined to sleep on in the coffin of their age, moved only by its petty controversies, preoccupations and vogues, that pass away within their own lives, leaving them in their old age distant viewers of the absurd wastage of youthful energies they once had. To live with the stream of time is to die daily, unwittingly, and never have hope of life.

Though the death of an age has long been prophesied, yet generations of men are reared and come to maturity as it heaves its death-throes. Richter, Blake and Shelley; Carlyle and Matthew Arnold; Nietzsche, Spengler and Toynbee: they and many more, all in one way or another, heard and proclaimed the death-knell. An empire reached its zenith, and fell within the period; a great nation arose, was defeated, arose again and again prepared its funeral pyre. New nations, new *ersatz* empires arose, poor imitations destined to be more ephemeral.

For nations themselves were passing; generalship, statesmanship, Thought itself. And as the very dregs rise up to take their brief curtain call, they find men like themselves buried ever more deeply in the passing moment, endeavouring to hold on to it.

What worm was that which worked through the might of Rome, over those long, seemingly interminable centuries we read of in Gibbon? After Marcus Aurelius, after the Antonines, why had it to take so long to die? How painful it is to see the adulterated empire throw up citizens of noble lineage but mean minds, grovelling for the sake of their silly estates before bearded barbarian conquerors whom their forefathers had kept as slaves. Gibbon blamed Christianity, but Carlyle saw the barbarian hordes as the scourge of God trampling out a world deep in vices at which the sun was sick. Genseric, Alaric, Attila – these half-savage, half-civilized men were raised by an avenging deity as horsemen of the apocalypse.

But the prospect of nemesis inspires not grandeur, not epic awe, but boredom – the event has been so long prophesied, and the interim has been filled up with triviality, and men have to live. So the world ends not with a bang but with a whimper, in prospect if not in fact. And paradoxically (or inevitably?), the last voice that will be listened to at such a time is the voice that pronounced the whole course of affairs almost in its entirety when it had scarce begun.

Writing of this, Shoghi Effendi has said: 'The destructive forces that characterize the [present order] should be identified with a civilization that has refused to answer to the expectation of a new age, and is consequently falling into chaos and decline.' Now Shoghi Effendi knew his Gibbon and Carlyle, but his assessment of the course of the modern age certainly does not derive from them. Frankly, who could have conceived of it, this frighteningly Judaic view of history, tempered by a visionary utopianism beyond the dreams of the most ardent millennialist? Did our epoch only know Shoghi Effendi as well as it knows Karl Marx, it certainly could not plead ignorance of its fate. For it is in the relatively brief writings of Shoghi

Effendi, heir to the prophetic wisdom of Bahá'u'lláh, and of 'Abdu'l-Bahá, that we find the weight of Bahá'í understanding of the times through which we now live. Possessing himself a vision of the course of history that spans the ringing grooves of change far into the future, Shoghi Effendi applied himself to the warnings and prophecies of the founders of the Bahá'í Faith, and gave us a modern eschatology.

The writings of Shoghi Effendi represent no considered, developed philosophy established over a given period of time, and treated in a succession of related volumes. In considering his articulation of the trends of modern society, we are compelled to remember the function he fulfilled as Guardian of the Bahá'í Faith. Yet it is not the aim of this chapter to view Shoghi Effendi's thought within the totality of his conception of the development of the Bahá'í Faith. This would require too vast a scope, and would call upon too great a knowledge for the present writer to acquit the task favourably. Shoghi Effendi's description of the modern apocalypse, as it is interpreted here, is thus necessarily a limited, edited version. Our concern is the immediate fate of humanity, albeit as seen through the mind of the second interpreter of the Bahá'í Revelation, a mind that draws its entire motivation and world picture from being steeped in the inspiration and training of this Revelation.

Although Shoghi Effendi, as author, wrote only two works, when taken as volumes conceived and composed as unified wholes, he wrote in addition many of his most memorable pieces in the form of letters to Bahá'í bodies and institutions. Such pieces, composed over a period spanning nearly the whole of his Guardianship (1922–57), have been collated into volume form, and so add to the corpus of his penmanship. There is no space here to discourse upon the Guardian's style; let it suffice to say Shoghi Effendi's writing represents a synthesis of a prodigious intellectual power, and a luminous spiritual vision. 'The individual has two wings,' the religious commentator Marcus Bach has recorded Shoghi Effendi as saying: 'knowledge and faith. When these are in perfect co-ordination, the soul rises to divine perfection.' The Spirit enlightens the intellect and the intellect expresses the mysteries of the Spirit: the synthesis demonstrates that love and reason, intelligence and ethics, are not divorced. Shoghi Effendi's prose is evidence of this truth; his theme expresses his saturation in the spirit of the Bahá'í Revelation, and his quotation from the Authors of the Bahá'í Faith, sometimes a single epithet of several words, at others a whole passage, is the core around which his argument is built, the skeleton-framework upon which he rears an edifice of substance comprehendable by the mind and soul. Words of erudition are used; lofty phrases and rolling sentences accrue in lengthy periods; but no word functions merely as rhetoric, each has its precise value in terms of the whole; meretriciousness is as foreign to his style as are the cliché and stale metaphor.

From the beginning, Shoghi Effendi juxtaposed, alongside his plans for the growth of the Bahá'í movement, observations on the state of the greater world in which it functioned. Thus he wrote, in 1924:

Disillusion and dismay are invading the hearts of peoples and nations, and the hope and vision of a united and regenerated humanity is growing dimmer and dimmer every day. Time-honoured institutions, cherished ideals, and sacred traditions are suffering in these days of bewildering change, from the effects of the gravest onslaught, and the precious fruit of centuries of patient and earnest labour is faced with peril. Passions, supposed to have been curbed and subdued, are now burning fiercer than ever before, and the voice of peace and good-will seems drowned amid unceasing convulsions and turmoil.[1]

The diagnosis he proffered at this stage was the same as he would for the rest of his life: 'Humanity, torn with dissension and burning with hate, is crying at this hour for a fuller measure of that love which is born of God, that love which in the last resort will prove the one solvent of its incalculable difficulties and problems.'[2] Then, as later, Shoghi Effendi was not content to deal in mere generalization, but gave particular instance of the grave illness he diagnosed:

1. *Bahá'í Administration*, p. 61.
2. ibid. p. 62.

'Nations, though exhausted and disillusioned, have seemingly begun to cherish anew the spirit of revenge [this, in 1924], of domination, and strife. Peoples, convulsed by economic upheavals, are slowly drifting into two great opposing camps with all their menace of social chaos, class hatreds, and worldwide ruin. Races, alienated more than ever before, are filled with mistrust, humiliation and fear, and seem to prepare themselves for a fresh and fateful encounter. Creeds and religions, caught in this whirlpool of conflict and passion, appear to gaze with impotence and despair at this spectacle of unceasing turmoil.'[3]

This would seem a very precise analysis of the forces arraying themselves in the mid-1920s, clear as it is in its forecast of a new world conflict following on the great events so recently ended.

In 1931, in one of his early open letters to the American Bahá'ís in which he expatiated at length on the significance of the growth of the Bahá'í Faith as against the dissolution of the greater world order, Shoghi Effendi accented his awareness of the hopeless plight of modern society. Taking as his text a quotation from 'Abdu'l-Bahá, in which he spoke of the coming dangers and prophesied greater ills than those experienced at the time [1920], Shoghi Effendi wrote:

Economic distress, since those words were written, together with political confusion, financial upheavals, religious restlessness and racial animosities, seem to have conspired to add immeasurably to the burdens under which an impoverished, a war-weary world is groaning. Such has been the cumulative effect of these successive crises, following one another with such bewildering rapidity, that the very foundations of society are trembling. The world, to whichever continent we turn our gaze, to however remote a region our survey may extend, is everywhere assailed by forces it can neither explain nor control.[4]

As in 1924, Shoghi Effendi was ready to point out the actual condition that supported his deep apprehensions:

The disquieting influence of over thirty million souls living under minority conditions throughout the continent of Europe; the vast and ever-swelling army of the unemployed with its crushing burden and demoralizing influence on governments and peoples; the wicked, unbridled race of armaments swallowing an ever-increasing share of

3. *Bahá'í Administration*, pp. 67–8.
4. 'The Goal of a New World Order', in *The World Order of Bahá'u'lláh*, pp. 30–31.

the substance of already impoverished nations; the utter demoralization from which the international financial markets are now increasingly suffering; the onslaught of secularism invading what had hitherto been regarded as the impregnable strongholds of Christian and Muslim orthodoxy – these stand out as the gravest symptoms that bode ill for the future stability of modern civilization.[5]

He proceeded, in a letter of 1936, to instance the 'signs of moral downfall' that accompanied the decline in religion, emphasizing that it was in this decline that the secret of the convulsions of the twentieth century was to be found.

With the Second World War, clearly foretold by Shoghi Effendi as we saw, he reiterated his belief that the ills facing world civilization were too radical to admit of amelioration. In 1941 he wrote:

The chief idols in the desecrated temple of mankind are none other than the triple gods of Nationalism, Racialism, and Communism, at whose altars governments and peoples, whether democratic or totalitarian, at peace or at war, of the East or of the West, Christian or Islamic, are, in various forms and in different degrees, now worshipping.[6]

Shoghi Effendi was under no illusions about the aftermath of the Second World War; whilst hailing the historic events occurring in San Francisco that led to the creation of the United Nations Charter, he did not expect this to prevent a future conflict between the post-War camps centred around the superpowers. He wrote, in 1948, of a world 'now hovering on the brink of a yet more crucial struggle'.[7] These indeed were the coldest days of the so-called 'Cold War' between East and West. Shoghi Effendi gave no indication – as indeed he had given no indication in 1924 – as to when the next struggle would occur; suffice to say that: 'Rumblings of catastrophes yet more dreadful agitate with increasing frequency a sorely stressed and chaotic world.'[8] Any return to economic prosperity must needs be temporary, for no theory of statesmanship, economics, or principle of moral inspiration could renew the

5. ibid. p. 32.
6. *The Promised Day Is Come*, pp. 117–18.
7. *Citadel of Faith*, p. 62.
8. ibid. p. 60.

ailing structure of world society. Shoghi Effendi voiced as early as 1931 a conviction that the course of immediate history was set for catastrophe. It was a sobering assessment, but was it any more than another prophecy of doom, taking its place among the many?

The central vision of Shoghi Effendi's writing is the emergence of the Faith of Bahá'u'lláh within a fast-declining world order that has failed to rise to the promise of the new age. The Bahá'í Faith is for him the repository of the creative power of the new age, a creative power born of divinity itself. The Divinity is the architect of human destiny, the Mover of history; human beings, though not thralls, are necessarily dependent on the revelatory source of progress and renewal which is channelled through the Divine Messenger from millennium to millennium. Man's response is not pre-determined: for in this consists his free-will. The course of modern history rests, for Shoghi Effendi, on mankind's reception of the Avatar of the new age in their midst. Their rejection of the twin Manifestations of God, the Báb and Bahá'u'lláh, has set into motion the forces of chaos and destruction so evident in the modern world. 'The powerful operations of this titanic upheaval', Shoghi Effendi wrote further of the process of change, 'are comprehensible to none except such as have recognized the claims of both Bahá'u'lláh and the Báb. Their followers know full well whence it comes, and what it will ultimately lead to.'[9]

This surprisingly forthright assertion might well educe protestation from the person but cursorily informed of Bahá'í belief: it is as crucial to the Bahá'í understanding of history as the theory of class struggle is to the Marxist's. Arguments can be made for the former, as for the latter; Shoghi Effendi's approach is hardly an exercise in polemics or the laying of ideological principle. If we turn to the most coherent expression of his reading of modern history – *The Promised Day Is Come*, written in 1941 – we can see how he carries his argument by dint of rhetoric, assertion, didacticism and sheer

9. *The Promised Day Is Come*, p. 2.

eloquence. A work of literature as well as an exegesis of Bahá'í belief, this view of the immediate history of our civilization demands acceptance or rejection on his own terms, rather like the Judaic masterpieces of the school of Old Testament prophecy, excepting that its grasp of historical detail is more exact.

The opening of *The Promised Day Is Come* is worth quotation for its literary excellence alone, for it not only condenses the critique of modern times that we have already observed in Shoghi Effendi's writing, it also recalls the classic eras when English prose was at its most aureate and resonant:

A tempest, unprecedented in its violence, unpredictable in its course, catastrophic in its immediate effects, unimaginably glorious in its ultimate consequences, is at present sweeping the face of the earth. Its driving power is remorselessly gaining in range and momentum. Its cleansing force, however much undetected, is increasing with every passing day. Humanity, gripped in the clutches of its devastating power, is smitten by the evidences of its resistless fury. It can neither perceive its origin, nor probe its significance, nor discern its outcome. Bewildered, agonized and helpless, it watches this great and mighty wind of God invading the remotest and fairest regions of the earth, rocking its foundations, deranging its equilibrium, sundering its nations, disrupting the homes of its peoples, wasting its cities, driving into exile its kings, pulling down its bulwarks uprooting its institutions, dimming its light, and harrowing up the souls of its inhabitants.[10]

This eloquent beginning may remind us of Gibbon in its use of the lengthy period and majestic cadence, and Carlyle in its prophetic fury, but the richness of its imagery and the force of its assonance and alliteration ('unprecedented' . . . 'unpredictable' . . . 'unimaginably' . . . 'ultimate' . . .) and repeated rhythms ('rocking its foundations, deranging its equilibrium, sundering its nations, disrupting the homes of its peoples' . . . etc.) recall the oriental idiom in which, as a Persian, Shoghi Effendi was saturated. It is fatal to aspire after grandeur and to fail, but to succeed means that one's argument is inevitably enhanced.

10. ibid. p. 1.

We shall return to the notion of judgement felt so ubiquitously in the work; but first we must establish the positive element in Shoghi Effendi's view of the apocalypse figured above – what lends it its 'unimaginably glorious . . . ultimate consequences'. What we find is a specific understanding of the Romantic idea of palingenesia, of death and re-birth, expressed in these terms:

We are indeed living in an age which, if we would correctly appraise it, should be regarded as one which is witnessing a dual phenomenon. The first signalizes the death-pangs of an order, effete and godless, that has stubbornly refused, despite the signs and portents of a century-old Revelation, to attune its processes to the precepts and ideals which the Heaven-sent Faith proffered it. The second proclaims the birth-pangs of an Order, divine and redemptive, that will inevitably supplant the former, and within Whose administrative structure an embryonic civilization, incomparable and world-embracing, is imperceptibly maturing. The one is being rolled up, and is crashing in oppression, bloodshed, and ruin. The other opens up vistas of a justice, a unity, a peace, a culture, such as no age has ever seen. The former has spent its force, demonstrated its falsity and barrenness, lost irretrievably its opportunity, and is hurrying to its doom. The latter . . . is plucking asunder its chains, and is vindicating its title to be the one refuge within which a sore-tried humanity, purged from its dross, can attain its destiny.[11]

In this passage the force of the new age, the age of promise, recreation and renewal, is entirely identified with the Bahá'í order growing up within the old world order it is to replace. The ideal of nineteenth-century seers, poets and philosophers has this precise an identification, and the dying order it replaces is the twentieth-century sequel to the nineteenth-century wasteland, or dark night. Several years before he wrote the above passage, Shoghi Effendi referred to the same concept of simultaneous, phoenix-like death and re-birth:

A twofold process . . . can be distinguished, each tending, in its own way and with an accelerated momentum, to bring to a climax the forces that are transforming the face of our planet. The first is essentially an integrating process, while the second is fundamentally disruptive. The former, as it steadily evolves, unfolds a System which

11. *The Promised Day Is Come*, p. 16.

may well serve as a pattern for that world polity towards which a strangely-disordered world is continually advancing; while the latter, as its disintegrating influence deepens, tends to tear down, with increasing violence, the antiquated barriers that seek to block humanity's progress towards its destined goal. The constructive process stands associated with the nascent Faith of Bahá'u'lláh, and is the harbinger of the New World Order that Faith must erelong establish. The destructive forces that characterize the other should be identified with a civilization that has refused to answer to the expectation of a new age, and is consequently falling into chaos and decline.[12]

The constructive forces alluded to are to be seen within the Bahá'í Administrative Order, as that order grows up within the world-wide Bahá'í community. The destructive forces are exactly those behind the modern apocalypse – the processes of war, famine, social strife and decay that we see all about us today. Only it is that the new world order remains to the bulk of mankind an unknown – the Bahá'í Faith an obscure sect originating in a reactionary oriental state. Yet in the hands of the writer we are discussing, how contrasting is his vision of the magnitude of this order and its Architect!

The discrepancy between the two assessments of the Bahá'í Revelation is really at the heart of *The Promised Day Is Come*. Nowadays, those who read the work are preponderantly Bahá'ís, who of course share the writer's faith, but who are in a miniscule proportion to the rest of the earth's inhabitants. Any outsider picking it up might find it turgid and pretentious in its theme. Once in history a few gathered to hear the earliest verses of the Koran from its channel, the Prophet Muhammad, and the majority of those laughed it to derision. Now the work is the holy book of millions, and has been so for more than a millennium; it was the same with the Gospels. This is the nature of religion – only history will look back from a later time and instruct us whether *The Promised Day Is Come* or the Book of Mormon has won the overwhelming assent that destiny gives to a handful of religious texts. If either one does, or if another in their place, we shall be able to say that this text

12. 'The Unfoldment of World Civilization', in *The World Order of Bahá'u'lláh*, p. 170.

has formed a millennium, and perhaps several civilizations in its image.

The tone of Shoghi Effendi's work is didactic and judgemental by nature of its thesis – that humanity's rejection of the Founders of the Bahá'í Faith has led directly to the nadir of human fortune in this century. The 'mighty wind of God' is itself the force of divine retribution on an errant century; in *The Promised Day Is Come* we see it indeed 'driving into exile . . . kings, pulling down . . . bulwarks, uprooting institutions', and so on. Here is an explanation of the dramatic fall of kingdoms and empires recorded by history since 1870. And here too is proffered an answer for those who are bewildered by the decline of ancient religions and the spread of secular power. At the centre of this inspired, unequivocal interpretation of modern history are two still largely unknown figures, so greatly revered by the author that many of the pages of his work are taken up with their words. Unknown even in their lives to the great mass of mankind, what they did and said is accorded the greatest significance; no more than the Book of Jeremiah does this work renege on its minority vision.

The vision of judgement we see contains, like the twofold process of death and rebirth, dual aspects: 'This judgement of God . . . is both a retributory calamity and an act of holy and supreme discipline. It is at once a visitation from God and a cleansing process for all mankind. Its fires punish the perversity of the human race, and weld its component parts into one organic, indivisible , world-embracing community. Mankind . . . is . . . being simultaneously called upon to give account for its past actions, and is being purged and prepared for its future mission.'[13] The judgement is therefore punishment tempered with far greater reward, for:

God, the Vigilant, the Just, the Loving, the All-Wise Ordainer, can, in this supreme Dispensation, neither allow the sins of an unregenerate humanity, whether of omission or of commission, to go unpunished, nor will He be willing to abandon His children to their fate, and refuse them that culminating and blissful stage in their

13. *The Promised Day Is Come*, pp. 2– 3.

long, their slow and painful evolution throughout the ages, which is at once their inalienable right and their true destiny.[14]

Though judgement is sure, this is not the judgement of a jealous Jehovah; humanity is being prepared for a new stage in its evolution, the 'culminating and blissful stage' in which it will emerge into a new state of being, as 'one organic, indivisible, world-embracing community'. To attain to this stage has been the 'true destiny' of man since his evolution began; this supreme state is moreover – unparalleled language in religion! – his 'inalienable right'. This is a new understanding of the Last Judgement indeed; we are reminded of Bahá'u'lláh's imponderable statement: 'My calamity is My providence, outwardly it is fire and vengeance, but inwardly it is light and mercy.'

Mankind, refusing to embrace the promise of the new day, ignores, calumniates, and persecutes the religious figures who bear its torch. Once again, it is the old story, he came unto his own, and his own received him not. The stories of the life-missions of the Báb and Bahá'u'lláh make poignant reading. Even the outsider, the non-believer, must be moved, especially if he has faith and is able to associate the sufferings of these two religious geniuses with the sufferings of his own Lord:

Unmitigated indifference on the part of men of eminence and rank; unrelenting hatred shown by the ecclesiastical dignitaries of the Faith from which it had sprung; the scornful derision of the people among whom it was born; the utter contempt which most of those kings and rulers who had been addressed by its Author manifested towards it; the condemnations pronounced, the threats hurled, and the banishments decreed by those under whose sway it arose and spread; the distortion to which its principles and laws were subjected by the envious and the malicious, in lands and among peoples far beyond the country of its origin – all these are but the evidences of the treatment meted out by a generation sunk in self-content, careless of its God, and oblivious of the omens, prophecies, warnings and admonitions revealed by His Messengers.[15]

Such a betrayal rests above all on the shoulders of the potentates, the men in authority. Carlyle's contempt for the

<hr>

14. ibid. p. 3.
15. ibid. pp. 5–6.

corrupt aristocracy of France in his *History of The French Revolution*: Marx and Engels's denunciations of the capitalist bourgeoisie – these are not more potent than Shoghi Effendi's concentrated, wholesale arraignment of the secular and ecclesiastical powers which he holds in the main responsible for the rejection of the new Faith. The mass of the peoples of Asia and Europe were shackled by the obscurantism of their political and religious masters from apprising themselves of the truth of the Bahá'í Revelation. Because of the opposition and indifference of these rulers, in the pithy words of Bahá'u'lláh himself: 'From two ranks amongst men power hath been seized: kings and ecclesiastics.'

The fate of the royal houses of Europe and of those of Turkey and Persia are dealt with at some length. It is historical fact that the birth of the Bahá'í Faith involved directly the Turkish and Persian empires of the period; the powerful monarchs of Europe also enter the chronicle because Bahá'u'lláh addressed to them singly and collectively Tablets informing them of his mission and admonishing them on their policies toward their peoples. Shoghi Effendi quotes extensively from these Tablets; then, having noted the negative response of all but one recipient, proceeds to point out the circumstances surrounding the fall of Louis Napoleon, Emperor of France (defeated at Sedan 1870); the humiliation of Pope Pius IX (confined to the Vatican by troops of King Victor Emmanuel II); the fall of the Romanovs (culminating in the events in Russia in 1917); the fall of the Hohenzollerns (culminating in the defeat of Germany in 1918 and abdication of Kaiser Wilhelm II); the collapse of the Habsburg Empire (dismembered at Versailles in 1919); the assassination of the Sultan of Turkey, 'Abdu'l-Aziz, and the eventual collapse of the throne of his successors (at the hands of Ataturk after the Great War); and the ending of the Persian Qájár dynasty (1925).

This is one of the most sombre and dramatic roll-calls of all history. It is of course well-known to the educated, but here is a commentator who sees the events it describes in a radically different way from the usual explanations. Of course the weaknesses of some of these monarchs and the empires they ruled (Turkey was the 'sick man of Europe', and the house of Habsburg an ill-fated dynasty from well into the nineteenth century) were widely recognized. But there was no greater shock in its time than the nemesis of the Buonaparte throne:

He who was actuated in provoking the Crimean War by his selfish desires, who was prompted by a personal grudge against the Russian Emperor, who was impatient to tear up the Treaty of 1815 in order to avenge the disaster of Moscow, and who sought to shed military glory over his throne, was soon himself engulfed by a catastrophe that hurled him in the dust, and caused France to sink from her preëminent station among the nations to that of a fourth Power in Europe.[16]

No history book as yet has recorded Louis Napoleon's retort to the warnings of a Persian exile in Ottoman domains – 'If this man is God, I am two gods!' Nor yet has one added the postscript that the exile foretold the great Emperor's fall in the same communication – 'For what thou hast done, thy kingdom shall be thrown into confusion, and thine empire shall pass from thine hands, as a punishment for what thou hast wrought.' The detached observer would be right to see the Emperor's fall as resulting from his overweening pride – and he would need to remember as well the wily sagacity of the Prussian Chancellor which provoked the conflict with France. Then what is the role of Bahá'u'lláh in the events in question? A direct causality would be hard to prove, but stranger still are the events pursuant to the Battle of Sedan in that *Annus Mirabilis*.

Pope Pius IX, described by Shoghi Effendi as: 'Authoritarian by nature, a poor statesman, disinclined to conciliation, determined to preserve all his authority,'[17] was also involved in the chain of events. He was bent upon establishing his authority by putting forward the dogma of papal infallibility. To him Bahá'u'lláh had addressed a tablet informing him that 'He Who is the Lord of Lords is come overshadowed with clouds', and had told the Pope to '"leave his palaces unto such as desire them", to "sell all the embellished ornaments" he possessed and

16. *The Promised Day Is Come*, pp. 52–3.
17. ibid. p. 54.

to "expend them in the path of God", and to "abandon his kingdom unto the kings", and emerge from his habitation with his face "set towards the Kingdom"'.[18]

Ignoring this summons, the Pope proceeded with his papal infallibility, summoning a General Council in Rome to make the declaration. A sizeable number of clergy were against such a move: 'Even so, they refused to vote for the decree,' says an eminent historian, 'but rather than cause scandal by voting against it they left Rome the day before . . . Thus when the final voting took place in St Peter's on 18 July 1870, amid a terrific thunderstorm, 533 voted for the decree, and only two against.' Then, the same writer continues: '*On the following day war was declared between France and Prussia*. At the beginning of August the French troops who guarded the Holy City were withdrawn from Rome. Early in September the Italian armies invaded the pope's territory, and later in the month the city capitulated, the kingdom of Italy was established, *and the temporal power of the papacy was at an end*.'[19] Although the Pope's declaration of infallibility in 1870 seemed to have no causal link with the ending of papal temporal power that followed soon after, we can see from this account that this loss of temporal power was intimately associated with the débâcle involving Louis Napoleon at Sedan. The fate of both men was interwoven, and both had defied the voice of Bahá'u'lláh. As Shoghi Effendi expresses it:

Rome 'the Eternal City, on which rest twenty-five centuries of glory,' and over which the Popes had ruled in unchallengeable right for ten centuries, finally became the seat of the new kingdom [of Italy], and the scene of that humiliation which Bahá'u'lláh had anticipated and which the Prisoner of the Vatican had imposed upon himself.[20]

The decline of both the Ottoman and Qájár dynasties was even more intimately associated with Bahá'u'lláh. The collapse of Ottoman power in the events leading up to and including the

18. *The Promised Day Is Come*, pp. 53–4.
19. Alec R. Vidler, *The Church in an Age of Revolution*, pp. 155–6 (italics mine).
20. *The Promised Day Is Come*, p. 55.

Great War is perhaps the most spectacular fall of all. This clearly was an abasement long overdue, and reading Bahá'u'lláh's Tablets to the Sultan and his references to Constantinople in others of his writings, there is no room for doubt that the Ottoman rulers' treatment of Bahá'u'lláh only compounded the accumulation of evils awaiting to befall this power in its hour of retribution. As for the rulers of Persia, the country which had done most to extirpate the Bahá'í Faith and its followers, their fate, like that of their Sunni antagonists in Turkey, was sealed by their sheer ineptitude and corruption.

The Pope still fulfilled a temporal role up to 1870, and the Sultan of the Ottoman Empire was also Caliph of Sunni Islam. The power that has been seized from ecclesiastics is, however, a feature of the greater decline that is the decline of religion itself. In Persia it was the Shí'i Muslim divines who were the most inveterate enemies of the new Faith. Bahá'u'lláh warned these same religious leaders not to treat the new Faith of God as their predecessors, the priests and doctors of the past, had treated Muhammad and Jesus Christ. The Bahá'í Faith, Shoghi Effendi emphasizes, was born into the Islamic world, whilst the majority of its non-Muslim followers, the adherents from the West, were of Christian origin. Whilst Bahá'u'lláh came to effect a religious renewal amongst mankind, he also pro-nounced the leaders of religion in every age guilty of hindering the ordinary people from 'attaining the shores of eternal salvation' because of their 'lust of leadership' and 'want of knowledge and understanding'. His works are replete with condemnations of the Muslim clergy, and berations of their ignorance and fanaticism. Shoghi Effendi instances in detail the remarkable decline of the fortunes of this clergy, particularly in Persia, but also further afield, most spectacularly in Turkey, where the state led an onslaught against orthodox religion, reversed the laws and practices of Islam and abolished the Caliphate: 'Strange, incredibly strange, must appear the position of this most powerful branch of the Islamic Faith, with no outward and visible head to voice its sentiments and convictions, its unity irretrievably shattered, its radiance obscured, its law undermined, its institutions thrown into hopeless confusion.'[21]

Bahá'u'lláh's Tablet to the Christian pontiff in Rome initiated a process of diminution of the power of Christian ecclesiastical orders that has gone on with increasing momentum to this day, according to Shoghi Effendi. 'Aided by the forces which the Communist movement has unloosed, reinforced by the political consequences of the last war [1914–18], accelerated by the excessive, the blind, the intolerant, and militant nationalism which is now convulsing the nations, and stimulated by the rising tide of materialism, irreligion, and paganism, this process is not only tending to subvert ecclesiastical institutions, but appears to be leading to the rapid dechristianization of the masses in many Christian countries.'[22] Few would disagree that the influence of the Christian Churches has declined by a massive degree in the wake of the secularizing trends of the twentieth century, and that the Christian spirit has suffered incalculably from the wars begun in Europe between so-called Christian states. The general dying out of religion, though occasioned to a great extent by the failure of the religious leaders to accept the revitalizing message of Bahá'u'lláh, according to Shoghi Effendi, nevertheless constitutes a fatal weakening of the social fabric. 'The greater the decline of religion, the more grievous the waywardness of the ungodly', explained Bahá'u'lláh.

Shoghi Effendi's interpretation of the symptoms of the modern age – its irreligion, its materialism, its conflicting ideologies and dangerous fanaticisms – would be acceptable to many. But why the insistence, to such a great degree, on the link between the decline in civilization that has set in, and the rejection or ignoring of the message of Bahá'u'lláh? Certainly, he does not insist on a dispensing with secondary causes to explain this decline – the process of secularism was well under way by the time Bahá'u'lláh gave his great summonses in the late 1860s and early 70s; the corruption and sheer backwardness

21. *The Promised Day Is Come*, p. 100.
22. ibid. p. 108.

of entities like the Ottoman and Habsburg Empires, and the
Qájár kingdom in Persia, surely ensured their eventual down-
fall. The great revolutionizing process in Europe that accompanied the new industrialization, and the growth in political
consciousness among the people, would both have meant sub-
stantial changes in the religious and political life of Europe if
Bahá'u'lláh had never sent a line to her crowned heads. Moreover, *The Promised Day Is Come* says little about the Far East or
indeed the role of America (although Shoghi Effendi dealt with
the latter question elsewhere, especially in his letters to the
American Bahá'ís). The work is in fact no potted historical
interpretation of the multifarious causes and effects discernible
in twentieth-century society, but a mighty glance into their
heart. The implication is that the coming of Bahá'u'lláh greatly
speeded up a process already in motion, and synchronized with
an age of the profoundest historical change. To borrow an
epithet from another historicist creed, history had reached one
of its 'critical points' – if we are to believe Shoghi Effendi, the
greatest critical point in the entire historical process, for this is
none other than the coming of age of the human race.

However, it is also true, as we have said in a previous chapter,
that the world of 1870–14 did not accept the principles which
Bahá'u'lláh then stated would conduce to its tranquillity. That
it did not lay down its armaments, convene a world conference
and establish a collective security, history attests only too
clearly. That in fact it has taken well nigh one hundred years for
human agencies to begin to think in universal terms and to
tackle the problems of mankind as though there was indeed
only one home – the entire earth – is painfully apparent, looking
back. The world has only recently caught up with and begun to
implement the wonderful principles of this remarkable
personage. Yet it might have done so much earlier – it might
have avoided two great wars, countless local wars and the final
catastrophic war which must surely be very near now. For as
late as 1984 individual governments are still attached to the
notion of national sovereignty, with all the connotations this
has for rivalries, the amassing of lethal armaments, and the

prevention of the solidarity of the entire human race from being achieved. When future generations, at peace, and wholly committed to the greater welfare of all mankind, look back at the historical period we have been discussing, and see that a call to peace and brotherhood was voiced by a lonely figure who was no more than a prisoner at the .time, but who saw far in advance of his contemporaries, they will surely canonize him as at least a remarkable genius. But because so many more of his teachings remain to the future for their fulfilment, and because men in those days will surely recognize the Spirit emanating from this source as too great to be that of a mere sage, we can perhaps guess that Shoghi Effendi's account of the late nineteenth and the twentieth centuries, as seen in *The Promised Day Is Come*, will be afforded a greater credence than now.

The Bahá'í view of modern history is of its time, growing out of a nineteenth-century background, but its significance stretches far into the future. It uses almost the same language to describe the new age as nineteenth-century European philosophers and poets. That this is no instance of plagiarism any researcher into the background to the Bahá'í Scriptures could verify. It might be that both are talking of the same phenomenon – it might be that where the thinkers leave off, the Bahá'í Faith expands into the vacuum to fulfil a stupendous promise.

There need be no shame in admitting that the Bahá'í Faith is an historicist creed, for it teaches a sense of history, a meaning for history and a goal to history – or it teaches nothing at all. For the believer in the Bahá'í Faith history has both a meaning and a goal, and he partakes in both. We must return to Shoghi Effendi to get a last view of the context in which we are working, and to see the modern apocalypse in its real import:

God's purpose is none other than to usher in, in ways He alone can bring about, and the full significance of which He alone can fathom, the Great, the Golden Age of a long-divided, a long-afflicted humanity. Its present state, indeed even its immediate future, is dark, distressingly dark. Its distant future, however, is radiant, gloriously radiant – so radiant that no eye can visualize it.[23]

23. op. cit. p. 120.

What we witness at the present time, during 'this gravest crisis in the history of civilization', recalling such times in which 'religions have perished and are born,' is the adolescent stage in the slow and painful evolution of humanity, preparatory to the attainment of the stage of manhood, the stage of maturity, the promise of which is embedded in the teachings, and enshrined in the prophecies of Bahá'u'lláh. The tumult of this age of transition is characteristic of the impetuosity and irrational instincts of youth, its follies, its prodigality, its pride, its self-assurance, its rebelliousness, and contempt of discipline.[24]

The world is, in truth, moving on towards its destiny. The interdependence of the peoples and nations of the earth, whatever the leaders of the divisive forces of the world may say or do, is already an accomplished fact. Its unity in the economic sphere is now understood and recognized. The welfare of the part means the welfare of the whole, and the distress of the part brings distress to the whole. The Revelation of Bahá'u'lláh has, in His own words, 'lent a fresh impulse and set a new direction' to this vast process now operating in the world. The fires lit by this great ordeal are the consequences of men's failure to recognize it. They are, moreover, hastening its consummation. Adversity, prolonged, world-wide, afflictive, allied to chaos and universal destruction, must needs convulse the nations, stir the conscience of the world, disillusion the masses, precipitate a radical change in the very conception of society, and coalesce ultimately the disjointed, the bleeding limbs of mankind into one body, single, organically united, and indivisible.[25]

24. ibid. p. 121.
25. ibid. p. 127.

Postscript

THE REALIZATION that unity, or the pursuit of it, either in national or international affairs, is the last thing men practise today, strengthened my intuition that the world is moving towards its ultimate catastrophe. Modern society is fatally sick, the process of decline discussed in this study is too deeply ingrained in civilization to be diverted by remedial measures. In 1984 has this situation, in essentials, changed for the better since 1934? The great issue of today is nuclear disarmament – can we, looking back at the failure of previous peace movements to prevent the nations going to war in 1914 and 1939, really hold out much hope for collective disarmament in the 1980s?

I appreciate the argument of the committed that an effort has to be made, that defeatism ensures the holocaust. Yet such a change of heart would be required – and so rapidly – that I cannot entertain the prospect of a miracle, given the habits and frames of mind that have brought us to the brink of extinction.

The death of the world in which we live has long been prophesied – and in its final death-throes (and we should remember these began in earnest in 1914 and have cost mankind millions of lives already) much of the population of our planet is now threatened. To face this awful reality one must perforce entertain some spiritual belief, some certitude in the indestructibility of the human spirit.

The ashes of the dying order of today must give rise to a phoenix-rebirth, in which the human race will emerge to build the world anew. The greatest struggle facing man is the establishment of a just world order, for human beings require order, organization and unity. The world of man is like a body, and that body must perform in perfect unity for the health of every individual part; likewise, the health of the parts must be procured before the whole can be at peace. There cannot be starvation and disease in one area, while another enjoys luxury.

We have to begin with the fundamentals before we can build the new order: governments only pay lip-service to the Charter of Human Rights of the United Nations, but to adhere to every point contained therein is no utopian ideal.

In the battle for this end, a change in the consciousness of our race is required. This is at heart a religious act, and could be greatly expedited by a genuine, universal religious revival. Religions of the past, if viewed in their purity, inculcated a brotherhood which united many. Today the world is compassed by religious strife. Religious disagreements, divisions and hatreds must cease to afflict the human race, for if the cure becomes a poison, it would be better to do without the cure. There is a spirit of religious tolerance in the world today, even amidst so much fanaticism and sectarianism. In the nineteenth-century Persian Prophet, Bahá'u'lláh, we can observe the highest standard of universalism and tolerance. He said: 'Let not a man glory in this, that he loves his country; let him rather glory in this, that he loves his kind.'

Loyalty to mankind as a whole must come first – patriotism, politics, loyalty to religion, come second. Political loyalties, as they are practised today, are a bane to the world. It seems that even where a political programme appears just and apposite to the needs of a given situation, political methods are themselves an actual evil. The reason is that politics pits man against man – in the future men may come to the conclusion that this kind of politics is both a reactionary and destructive force, no matter what its ideological ingredient.

The Bahá'í Faith is both a religion and a system of organization. It has been likened to an organic structure that develops from the embryo until it encompasses, in its maturity, the entire environment in which it grew. The seed-bed of the Bahá'í religion today, less than one hundred and fifty years after its inauguration, is the whole earth. Bahá'í teachings range over the whole spectrum of man's material and spiritual life; they provide for his education, at the same time enabling him to function in his society. They allow for the evolution of man, through his society, into a collective entity. Both within man, and without, the Bahá'í teachings have the power to originate a new creation: the new phoenix emerging from the ashes of man's inchoate historical past.

Select Bibliography

General

BARRACLOUGH, GEOFFREY. *An Introduction to Contemporary History*. Harmondsworth, 1967.

BURY, JOHN B. *The Idea of Progress*. London, 1920.

CARLYLE, THOMAS. *Critical and Miscellaneous Essays*. Vols I–IV, London, 1872.

— *Sartor Resartus*. London, 1897.

—*The French Revolution*. 3 vols, London, 1896.

— *On Heroes and Hero-Worship*. London, 1897.

— *The Latter-Day Pamphlets*. London 1897.

COLLINGWOOD, ROBIN G. *The Idea of History*. Oxford, 1951.

DE CHARDIN, TEILHARD. *The Future of Man*. London, 1969.

GARDINER, PATRICK L. (ed.). *Theories of History*. New York, 1959.

— (ed.). *The Philosophy of History*, London, 1974.

GAY, P. J. *The Enlightenment: an interpretation*. 2 vols, London 1970.

GOETHE, J. W. VON. *Wilhelm Meister's Apprenticeship and Travels*. Trans. T. Carlyle, 2 vols, London, 1899.

HERDER, J. G. *Reflections on the Philosophy of the History of Mankind*. Abr. F. E. Manuel, Chicago, 1968.

HUXLEY, ALDOUS. *Brave New World*. Harmondsworth, 1955.

KOESTLER, ARTHUR. *Darkness at Noon*. Harmondsworth, 1964.

LESSING, G. E. *The Laocoon and other Prose Writings*. Trans. W. B. Rönnfeldt, London, 1895.

MARX, KARL, & ENGELS, FRIEDRICH. *The Communist Manifesto*. Harmondsworth, 1967.

MILLER, HENRY. *The Air-Conditioned Nightmare*. London, 1973.

— *Tropic of Capricorn*. London, 1966.

ORWELL, GEORGE. *Animal Farm*. Harmondsworth, 1951.

— *Nineteen Eighty-Four*. Harmondsworth, 1954.

— *Inside the Whale and other Essays*. Harmondsworth, 1962.

ORWELL, GEORGE. *Decline of the English Murder and other Essays*. Harmondsworth, 1965.

RENAN, ERNEST. *The Life of Jesus*. London, 1935.

TOYNBEE, ARTHUR J. *An Historian's Approach to Religion*. London, 1956.

— *A Study of History*. Abr. D. Somervell, 2 vols, London, 1946.

— *Civilization on Trial*. London, 1948.

VIDLER, ALEC R. *The Church in an Age of Revolution, 1789 to the Present Day*. Harmondsworth, 1971.

The Bábí and Bahá'í Religions

'ABDU'L-BAHÁ. *Some Answered Questions*. Rev. ed., Wilmette, Illinois, 1981.

BALYUZI, H. M. *Edward Granville Browne and the Bahá'í Faith*. London, 1970.

— *The Báb*. Oxford, 1973.

BROWNE, EDWARD G. *Materials for the Study of the Bábí Religion*. Cambridge, 1918.

CURZON, GEORGE N. *Persia and the Persian Question*. London, 1892.

MOMEN, MOOJAN. *The Bábí and Bahá'í Religions, 1844–1944*. Oxford, 1981.

NASH, GEOFFREY P. *Iran's Secret Pogrom – the Conspiracy to Wipe out the Bahá'ís*. Sudbury, Suffolk, 1982.

SHOGHI EFFENDI. *Bahá'í Administration*. Wilmette, Illinois, 1968.

— *Citadel of Faith*. Wilmette, Illinois, 1970.

— *God Passes By*. Wilmette, Illinois, 1970.

— *The Dawnbreakers – Nabíl's Narrative*. London, 1953.

— *The Promised Day Is Come*. Rev. ed., Wilmette, Illinois. 1981.

— *The World Order of Bahá'u'lláh*. Wilmette, Illinois, 1955.

TOWNSHEND, GEORGE. *The Promise of All Ages*. London, 1934.